Treasured Wrappings

Gift Packages to Give and Give Again

Krause Publications
700 East State St., Iola, WI 54990-0001
Telephone (715) 445-2214
www.krause.com

Please call or write for our free catalog of publications. Our toll-free number to place an order or obtain a free catalog is 800-258-0929 or please use our regular business telephone 715-445-2214 for editorial comment and further information.

Printed in the United States of America

Library of Congress Catalog Number: 99-62866

ISBN: 0-87341-840-9

Table of Contents

Introduction

by Karen Ancona
Editor, *CNA* magazine

This book will change every special occasion in your life. It's about starting a new tradition and possibly a new hobby; it's about gift giving; about saving trees and recycling; and it's about exploring your creative nature.

All of these topics are wonderfully wrapped up in, you guessed it, making your own gift wrapping and gift boxes! In some instances, you'll be crafting paper and fabric wrappings for boxes. Other times, you will decorate directly on box tops. There's the added benefit (besides the fun of it all) that these projects will put an end to those awful searches for boxes to hold impossibly shaped gifts like basketballs and roller skates. Now you can sew a gift bag that will make any gift presentable and beautiful.

The ultimate aim of this book is to get you started on a lifelong hobby that will take you far beyond the projects we've included. Best of all, you need no special talent to begin your new hobby. There's no previous experience required! Even very young children can make special gift packages. In fact, the first handmade gift package that I received was created by a nine-year-old.

Create a Memory

Before I reached school age, my sister, who is four years my senior, delighted me one Christmas with the gift of a seashell she had painted and then sprinkled with glitter. She presented it to me inside a small box she had decorated with a typical one-dimensional drawing of ocean waves and blue sky. A cutout paper boat stood atop its lid. Inside the box, the shell nestled in a bed of sand mixed with loose glitter. It was a spectacular girt for me at age five, and the memory is still spectacular for me at midlife. I recall the reflection of the Christmas tree lights on the glittering bed of sand and the new respect I gained for my sister, who instantly became a clever artist in my opinion.

Before that Christmas day ended, I had spilled the glitter and sand on the living room carpet. We retrieved as much of it as we could, but the magic beach inside the box was never the same. I don't know what finally became of the shell. The decorated box, however, still exists, and sits in my dresser drawer of odd treasures. The paper-boat-topping has been reduced to an unrecognizable lump. But the sight of the box, - with its primitive sea scene - always causes me to smile and prompts a phone call to my sister, who now lives miles and miles away from me.

I suppose it's safe to say that I've always been impressed with gift wrappings. Over the years, this fascination has made me a collector of sorts - of unusual boxes, package adornments, and fancy papers. These, along with novelty fabrics and even colorful feathers, artificial flowers, and sewing notions, are my stash of supplies for adding a personal touch to every gift I give.

Start a Tradition

What adds to my interest is that as I've expanded my list of supplies for creating wrappings and become more creative in my endeavors, others have joined in my "hobby" with enthusiasm. Most special family occasions that call for gift giving are preceded by a day of crafting gift wraps and decorating plain boxes. Grandchildren as young as four and five join in. Remember, there are no mistakes in this hobby! Plain paper or white box lids come to life just as delightfully with advanced skills as with four-year-old crayon markings. Rubber stamping makes artists out of all of us. And sewing a gift bag requires very little skill. A straight stitch will do the trick.

The results of these crafting gatherings is that I now receive as many creative packages as I give, and I enjoy a collection of personally decorated boxes, handmade gift bags, and fancy gift toppers. What fun it is to reuse those projects next year on someone else's family gift! I encourage you, as I've encouraged my family members, to sign and date your wrapping creations. As we pass these wrappings around from occasion to occasion, there's lots of lively conversation. Everyone loves to remember who made what, when. And children love to see how their crafting skills have improved over time.

In a true spirit of recycling, I've managed to convert some of the sturdiest decorated boxes I have received into other things. I've transformed small decorated boxes into paper clip holders and larger boxes made to hold cookies into sewing boxes. These are displayed around my home. The entire cycle of making, giving, and receiving has become a tradition for our family and circle of close friends. Everyone tells me that they anxiously anticipate the wraps as well as the gifts.

My profession as editor of a trade magazine for the craft industry keeps me in touch with the interesting new papers, ribbons, clays, fabrics, paints, dyes, and "stuff" that can be used, with a little creative spirit, to make very personal and unique gift presentations. That fortunate circumstance and my concern for the environment (I shudder to think of how many trees end up in garbage bags each Christmas morning as literally tons of wrapping paper is torn off gifts and thrown away) were the inspiration behind my suggestion to Krause Publications to publish an "idea" book on creative gift wrappings. I was happy to learn that I'm not alone in my appreciation of what goes outside a gift box as well as what rests inside and in my concern for the trees. Krause jumped on the idea and the result is this book chock full of great projects.

We've deliberately chosen projects for this book that use a wide variety of products. Some of them you may already have in your home, but others can be purchased at a local craft or fabric store. I'm certain that as you shop for supplies, you'll be tempted to add a bit of this and that to your creation. Do it! That's the fun of going "beyond" traditional wrapping paper and ribbons. Your gifts can reflect your personality and creative talents. Though our designers offer wonderful projects, let them serve as entry into creative gift wrap. Eventually, you'll want to "take off" on your own ideas. Soon your projects will carry a very personal signature.

Contrary to many cultures where tradition sets the guidelines for gift wrapping, we hope you will explore many avenues of creativity. We've learned that in Japan, the color of ribbons or ties has its own special meaning. Sometimes special paper-folding techniques translate into special messages. For example, some people believe all raw edges of wrapping paper should be folded under so the gift recipient's "luck" is not cut. Superstition? Whatever. It's fun to follow tradition, but it's also fun to set your own family tradition and step outside the "norm."

Karen Ancona

Betty's Beginner Project

Betty Auth

Betty's main areas of design interest are woodburning, colored pencil work, crazy quilting, and embellishment. She is very interested in reviving vintage hand arts. Betty writes a regular column for Arts & Crafts Magazine.

"In the Garden" Book Box

If you can neatly wrap a package, you can make this simple book box. It is covered with natural handmade paper available at craft stores everywhere. Substitute gift wrapping paper or wallpaper or paint the box with acrylic paint. The box is embellished with silk flower petals that have been removed from the stem, and although this one features a poppy, you can use your favorite flower. You'll find lots of bugs in the toy section of your local discount store or the floral section of the craft store. Choose a friendly one and add leaves and beads or buttons.

Instructions:

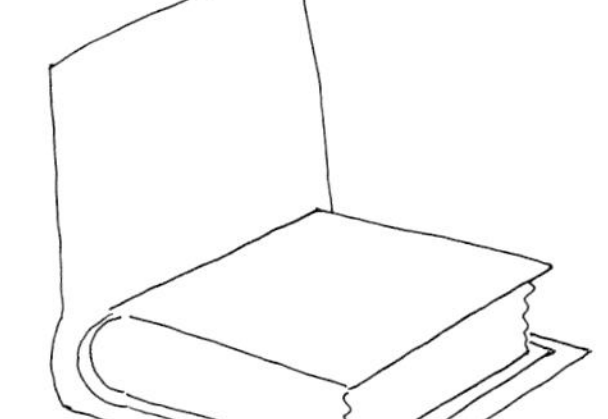

1. Lay the handmade paper face down on the work surface. Place the box on the wrong side of the paper and trace around it with a pencil, leaving a 1/2" margin all around. Carefully cut it out.

2. Working with one section of the box at a time, spread glue uniformly over the bottom of the box and set it on the paper, pressing it in place. Smooth the paper with your fingertips, working from the center out. Continue wrapping the paper around the spine of the box, then the top, spreading the glue and pressing. Weight the box while the glue dries, then wrap the 1/2" paper margins around the edges of the book, gluing well. If the paper is too wide for the edges, wait for the glue to dry, then trim off the excess with a craft knife.

3. Cut a 7-1/2" x 5-1/2" piece of lining fabric and turn under 1/4" on each edge, making the finished piece 5" x 7". Press and trim away the excess fabric at each corner so it lays flat. Glue the fabric inside the box lid, keeping it clear of the box hinge.

4. Glue the leaf spray on the lid at an angle and glue the wooden beads on top as berries. Glue five gold beads on and around the wooden ones. Glue the bug on top of a leaf.

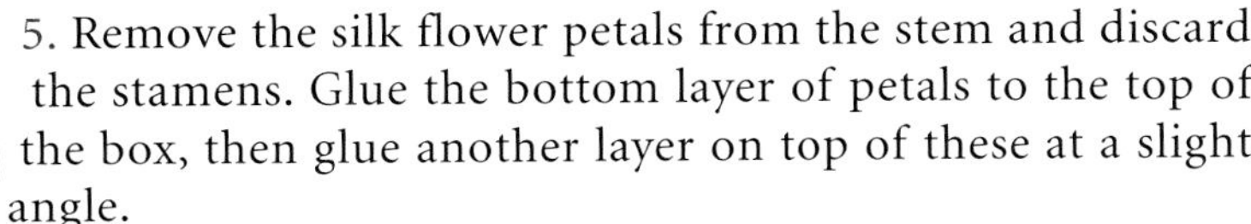

5. Remove the silk flower petals from the stem and discard the stamens. Glue the bottom layer of petals to the top of the box, then glue another layer on top of these at a slight angle.

6. String the bead chips on some bead thread and pull them in a circle, tying the ends of the thread together tightly. Put a drop of glue on the thread knot and let it dry, then clip the thread ends. Nestle the bead chip cluster in the center of the flower and glue it in place. Glue the remaining gold beads around the chips.

7. Fold under each end of the ribbon and glue. Glue the ribbon to the bottom of the box and glue Velcro on the box lid and the other end of the ribbon to hold the box closed. Glue the small button on the top of the ribbon.

The following products were used for this project: Aleene's Thick 'n Tacky Designer Glue.

Materials:

Paper maché book box, 5" x 7-1/2" x 3"
10" x 16" sheet natural handmade paper
7" x 10" fabric for lid lining
9" orange ribbon, 1"-wide
1/2" orange button
Velcro cut and loop tape
5-leaf spray beige velvet leaves
Ladybug
Beads:
5 round flat wooden beads
30 00mm round gold beads
30 natural stone chip beads
Bead thread
4-1/2" silk poppy
Tacky glue
Scissors
Craft knife
Ruler

Betty's Intermediate Project

Embellished Slide Box

Use your choice of trims and embellishments on a simple photo slide box.

In keeping with the "waste not, want not" philosophy, convert commonly found boxes like these photo slide boxes into beautiful and fanciful gift holders for small items. The coverings consist of ribbon scraps, pieces of lace, beads, buttons, or silk ribbon roses. Substitute charms or buttons for some of the beads or ask a friend for a broken necklace and use the beads to make her a very special gift box.

The instructions are for the lavish red box. Once you see how it's done, use your imagination to vary the trims and embellishments like I did on the black box and the fabric-covered box.

Instructions:

1. Measure the ribbon and cut two pieces to fit around the outside of the box lid and the box bottom, with a slight overlap on each piece. Spread glue evenly along one side of the lid and lay the ribbon on the glue, smoothing it along the side. Continue around the lid, trimming and overlapping the ends. Repeat for the box bottom. Set aside to dry.

2. To dye the doily, place several layers of paper towels on the work surface. Wash the doily to remove sizing, rinse well, and wring out. Lay the damp doily on the paper towels and drizzle red dye sparingly into the center. Use a paintbrush to spread the dye toward the outside edge, leaving about 1/2" undyed. The dye will spread and run a little, fading out and blurring. If the line is too defined, wet the brush and drip more water on the edge. Set the doily aside to dry or iron it between several paper towels (don't crush the fibers).

3. When the doily is dry, attach the beads as follows:

a. Thread the needle with 18" Nymo thread and knot the end. Choose the side of the doily you want to face up (one side will be more colorful than the other). Beginning at the edge where there is a picot or "point," come up from the back to hide the knot and take a small stitch.

b. Thread on one elongated bead, one larger round or square bead, and one small opaque bead. Go around the small bead, then back up through the other two and take another small stitch in the doily. Pull securely but not tight enough to cause the bead string to bunch up. Repeat, attaching bead strings about every 1/2" all around the doily.

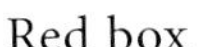

Red box

Black box

Black box

4. Spread a layer of glue evenly over the top of the box and center the doily on it, pressing it down into the glue. Dab some glue under the doily on each side and the end of the box to hold it firmly.

5. Glue the large button in the center of the doily with lots of glue and firmly press it down.

6. Tuck a piece of fancy fabric in the bottom of the box.

The following products were used for this project: Delta Quik 'n Tacky White Glue, Delta Brush-On Dye, Nymo Beading Thread.

Materials:

Plastic slide box, 3-1/4" x 2 -1/4" x 2-1/8"
24" burgundy satin ribbon, 1"-wide
5" round pineapple doily, white or off-white
Red fabric dye
Small round paintbrush
Beads:
20 clear red glass elongated beads, 1/2"-3/4"
20 clear red round or square beads, 1/4"
20 opaque red glass round beads, 4mm-6mm
Scrap of silk or velvet for inside box
Tacky glue
Nymo beading thread
Beading needle
1-1/2" red decorative button or two buttons stacked together

Betty's Advanced Project

Hooray Cowboy Woodburned Box

This box is designated as advanced because it requires two separate craft techniques - woodburning and beaded embellishment. If it were made with additional woodburned star medallions on the top instead of the beaded buckle, it would be less complicated. Either way, it's the perfect container for a boy's gift. Imagine what interesting treasures a young man would keep in it after the gift is removed.

Instructions:

1. Trace the patterns on tracing paper and lightly tape them in place on the box. Slip the graphite paper (graphite facing the wood) under the patterns and trace with a #2 pencil. It's helpful to tape the box closed before transferring the patterns. Remove the tracing paper and go over the lines with a pencil if necessary.

2. Follow the manufacturer's safety instructions for inserting the tip and heating the woodburner. Tape the wire holder to the work surface and rest the woodburner on it when not in use. Hold the woodburner as you would hold a pen and go over the pencil lines very slowly. The darkness of the burning is controlled by the length of time the point touches the wood, so keep the point moving or lift it from the surface so it won't make an unwanted dot. Outline all the designs with the woodburner. Darken and fill in the designs using hatching, scribbling, and stippling (refer to photo).

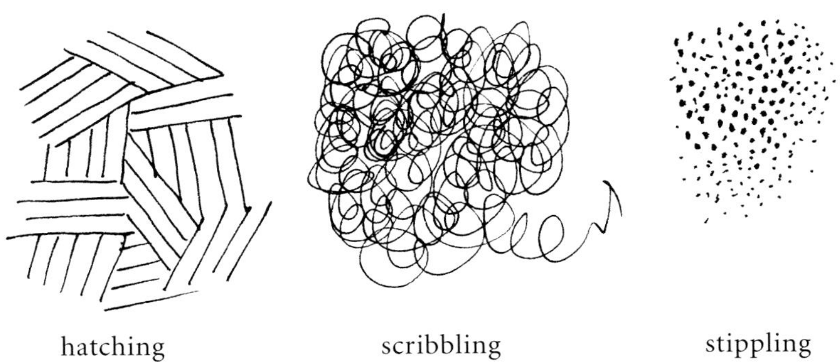

3. Erase all the graphite and pencil marks and very lightly sand off all the eraser marks. Stain the box inside and out with a mixture of half walnut gel stain and half clear glaze base. Brush the mixture on one surface, then rub off the excess with a lint-free cloth. Continue staining all surfaces evenly and let dry.

4. Apply two coats of matte varnish, allowing to dry and sanding very lightly between coats.

Beaded Embellishment

A different buckle may be substituted, since this one is a flea market find. Just make sure the size is no larger than 2" across the bar.

1. Cut 7" lengths of ribbon in four different colors. Insert one end of a ribbon through the hole in an arrowhead bead, bring the end up about 1/2" and glue the end to the ribbon, securing the bead in the loop. Repeat for the other three ribbons. Let dry for about five minutes.

Materials:

Basswood box ,
10-3/4" x 7 -1/4" x 2-1/4"
Woodburner with Mini-Flow point
Walnut gel wood stain
Clear glaze base
Matte acrylic varnish
Medium sandpaper
3/4" flat white nylon paint-brush
Lint-free cloth
Masking tape
Tracing paper
Graphite paper
#2 pencil
Bead & buckle embellishment:
- *1-1/2"square plastic belt buckle*
- *1-3/4" round scalloped leather medallion (or 2" felt circle)*
- *4mm silk ribbon: pale blue, turquoise, pale pink, tangerine, yellow*

Beads:
- *12 amber frosted glass arrowhead beads*
- *8 assorted 8mm-10mm round or pony beads to match ribbons*
- *8 assorted 6mm-8mm round or square beads to match ribbons*
- *8 small gold donut beads*

2. Lay out the sequence of beads for each of the four ribbons. Choose a ribbon and begin threading it as follows:

a. Thread the free end of the ribbon through a large-eyed 8mm-10mm bead and push it gently down to the top of the arrowhead bead, covering the raw end of the ribbon where it is glued. If necessary, trim the ribbon end to hide it.

b. Add a 6mm-8mm bead. Go through the hole of a gold donut bead and slide it down to 1/2" from the first two beads.

c. Move the ribbon around the outside of the donut, through the hole, around the outside again, and back through the hole. This should secure it on the ribbon.

d. Add another 6mm-8mm bead, then another donut bead, securing as before, then the final 8mm-10mm bead. Lay the strand aside and repeat for the other three ribbons.

3. Insert one ribbon over the buckle bar from the front, wrap the end around to the back, and glue to the back of the ribbon so it hangs over the bar. Repeat for the three remaining ribbons. Allow the glue to dry.

4. Bring the ribbons together about 1/2" above the last beads and braid loosely for about 1/2".

5. String seven arrowhead beads on a 6" length of yellow ribbon. Place one end of the ribbon over the buckle bar, outside the first four ribbons, and glue as before. Make a garland of the arrowhead beads that will hang just below the buckle, then secure the opposite end of the garland to the other side of the bar. Let the glue dry.

6. Trim all the ribbon ends at the back of the buckle, then glue the whole buckle to the leather medallion. Apply some weight and let it dry until the ribbons are secure, then glue the medallion to the box.

The following products were used for this project: Walnut Hollow Basswood Keepsake Box #3211, Walnut Hollow Creative Woodburner #5567, Walnut Hollow Mini-Flow Point #5593, Delta Walnut Gel Wood Stain, Delta Clear Faux Glaze Base, Delta Acrylic Matte Varnish, Loew-Cornell 3/4" Flat White Nylon Paintbrush #798.

Enlarge horse and rider 200%

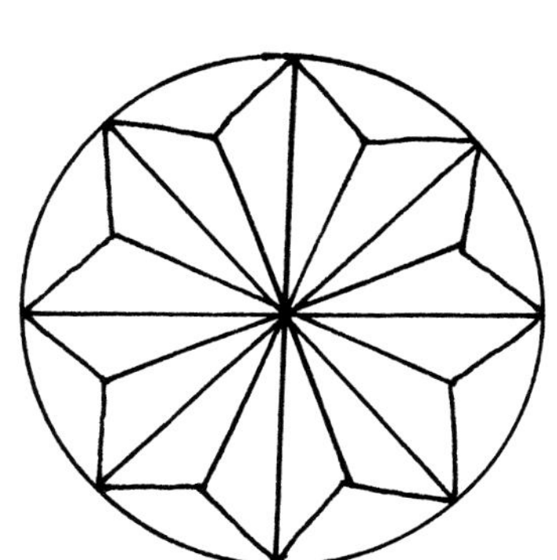

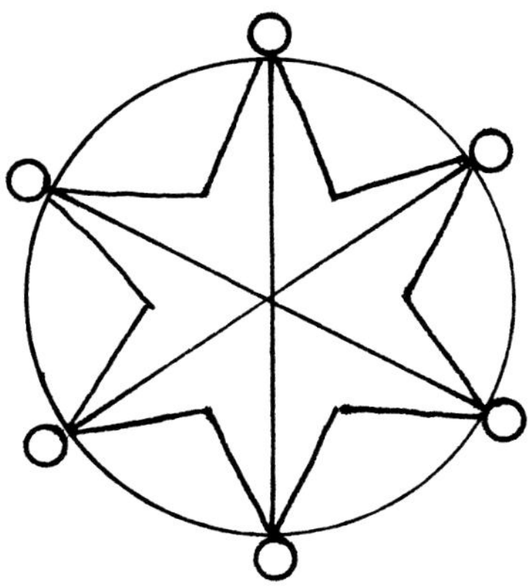

Joyce's Beginner Project

Joyce Bennett

Joyce is the host of the television series Naturally Floral, *and author of many craft books. She has been involved in the craft industry for over 30 years and particularly enjoys teaching craft projects to enthusiasts of all ages.*

MilleFlora Gift Ball

Decorate a break-apart clear plastic ball with pressed flowers from your garden. To use the ball, wrap a small present, place it inside the ball, and tie the ball with a pretty ribbon. Be sure to tell the recipient to fill the ball with potpourri after the gift is removed.

Instructions:

1. Using repositionable adhesive, lightly spray the faces of the pressed flowers and foliage. Arrange the flowers and foliage on the inside halves of the ball with the flower faces against the ball facing outward so you see the faces from the outside when the ball halves are put together.

2. Place a single ply of facial tissue inside each half of the ball, covering the flowers. To make the tissue fit, cut slits from each corner to the center of the tissue and overlap. Dab glue inside the halves of the ball and gently spread it with the brush. Let dry.

The inside of the ball after the gold paint is applied.

3. Apply gold acrylic paint to the insides of the halves of the ball and let dry. Put the two halves together and trim with a bow or raffia.

The following products were used for this project: Delta Stencil Magic Repositionable Stencil Spray Adhesive, Delta Ceramcoat Gleams 14K Gold Acrylic Paint, Delta Sobo Premium Craft & Fabric Glue.

Materials:

Break-apart clear plastic ball
Pressed flowers and foliage (I used pansies and ferns)
Facial tissue
Repositionable stencil spray adhesive
Gold acrylic paint
Craft & fabric glue
Soft 1/2" brush
Ribbon or raffia for trim

Joyce's Intermediate Project

Laminated Botanical Bags

Start with materials found around the house, add a little glue and a touch of gold and you'll have a great way to package almost anything!

Instructions:

9" Bag

1. Cut a 12" x 18" rectangle of brown paper.

2. Spray the brown paper lightly with repositionable adhesive spray and let it dry. Position the flowers, foliage, and moss on the bag in the design of your choice.

3. Separate some two-ply facial tissues into single layers. Place this over the pressed flowers, foliage, and moss, completely covering the brown paper. Dribble fabric glue all over the tissue. Use the soft brush to spread the glue as evenly as possible. The tissue will wrinkle up, creating a textured look. Let dry.

4. Using the sponge or your finger, apply gold acrylic paint to the raised surfaces of the design and let it dry.

5. Using the brush, apply the varnish and let it dry.

6. Shape the paper in a tube by overlapping the two longest edges by 1". Glue with tacky glue and let dry. Form a bag shape from the tube by creasing the corners in the bag so the tube forms a rectangle. Fold in the bottom sides and bottom edges of the front and back of the bag so they touch. Glue a rectangle of brown paper over the bottom of the bag. Set the bag upright and place a weight inside it while it dries.

7. To make the handles, punch two holes on each side of the bag and thread with ribbon, raffia, or cord. Tie knots in the ends of the ribbon to secure.

6" Bag

1. Cut a 7" x 10" rectangle of brown paper with the decorative edged scissors.

2. Follow steps 2 through 5 above to laminate the paper.

3. Form a tube shape by overlapping the two longest edges of the bag by 1". Glue the overlap together with tacky glue and let dry.

4. Decide which is the top and bottom of the bag. Round the bottom edge of the bag with scissors. Fold the rounded edges over one another and glue together. Let dry.

5. To make the handles, punch two holes on each side of the bag and thread with ribbon, raffia, or cord. Tie knots in the ends of the ribbon to secure.

Materials:

Brown paper (grocery bag, lunch bag, etc.)
Pressed flowers and foliage
Spagnum moss
Soft 1/2" brush
Facial tissue
Repositionable stencil adhesive spray
Craft & fabric glue
Gold acrylic paint
Satin exterior varnish
Tacky glue
Sponge
Decorative edged scissors (optional)
Ribbon, raffia, or cord for handles

Pocket Purse

1. Trace the pattern on the back of a 7" square of laminated brown paper (see steps 2 through 5 for the 9" bag on page 17 for laminating instructions). Follow the instructions on the pattern and glue the outer flaps to the inside of the purse with tacky glue. Glue the purse at the base and down the open side.

2. Glue the cord inside the purse for the handle.

The following products were used for this project: Delta Stencil Magic Repositionable Stencil Spray Adhesive, Delta Ceramcoat Gleams 14K Gold Acrylic Paint, Delta Sobo Premium Craft & Fabric Glue, Delta Ceramcoat Satin Exterior Varnish, Delta Quik 'n Tacky Glue.

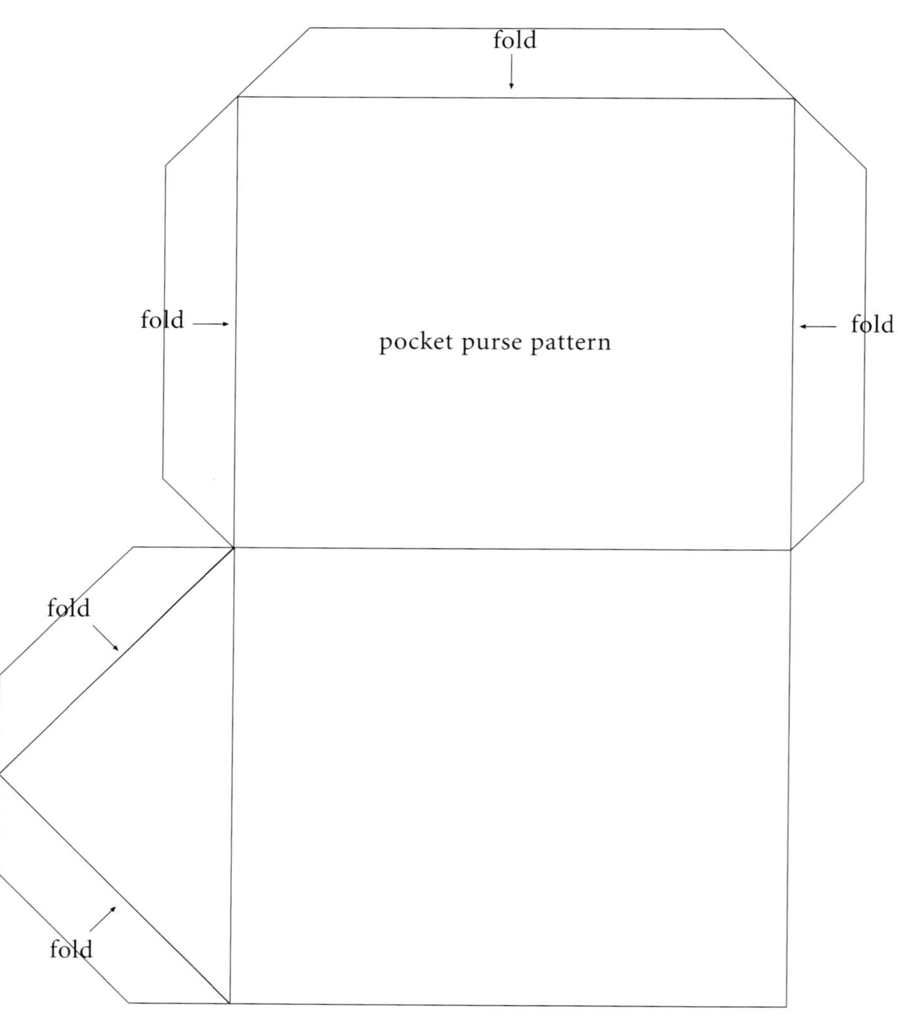

Topiary Wreath Box

Joyce's Advanced Project

Use lace, paint, glue, dried flowers, and foliage to create a lovely gift box from a paper mache´ box. I chose a 9″ oval, but you might like a different shape or size. The process is the same, no matter what size or shape you use.

Materials:

9" oval paper maché box with lid
26" any color lace, 3"-wide
26" any color lace, 1"-wide
Acrylic paint:
Silver Pine, 14k Gold
Craft & fabric glue
Satin exterior varnish
Brush
Sponge
1 oz. eucalyptus leaves and tips
Moss (any variety)
Dried or preserved flowers of your choice

Instructions:

1. Glue the 3"-wide lace around the box sides and let dry. Glue the 1"-wide lace around the rim of the box lid and let dry.

2. Lightly sponge two coats of green paint on the outside and inside of the box and lid, allowing to dry between coats.

3. Lightly sponge two coats of gold paint on the outside and inside of the box and lid, allowing to dry between coats.

4. Apply one coat of varnish and let dry.

5. Glue moss in an oval frame around the top of the box lid, using the photo as a guide. Glue eucalyptus leaves and flowers or foliage of your choice to the moss. Let dry.

6. Sponge gold acrylic paint on the leaves. *Hint: To maintain the softness and color of the foliage, lightly spray with clear acrylic spray.*

7. Add your choice of ribbon to finish the box.

The following Delta products were used for this project: Ceramcoat Acrylic Paints, Ceramcoat Gleams Acrylic Paint, Sobo Premium Craft & Fabric Glue, Ceramcoat Satin Exterior Varnish.

Fringed Folio

This "box" is ideal for a book or other flat gift such as a framed photo or memory book under 1" thick. It utilizes a plastic file envelope purchased at an office supply store as its base. You can use various types of home decorating fabric remnants and embellish them with photos, fabric paint, charms, jewels, or stencils - but don't forget the tassels or fringe! There are limitless options to this basic design.

Cari's Beginner Project

Cari Clement

Cari has been involved in fiber from the age of eight, when she started knitting. Her design career officially began in 1981, when she first designed sweaters for magazines and yarn companies and manufactured her own line of knitwear. She is now president of CC Product Co./Bond America, manufacturers of knitting machines, threads, punch needle embroidery tools, kits, and the Tassel Magic tassel and fringe making tool.

Materials:

10" x 12" plastic file folder
1/2 yard decorating fabric
1 ball each rayon chenille: Hunter Green, Deep Red
1 ball gold rayon crochet thread
2 star charms
Tacky glue
Fabric glue
Paper clips
Trim Tool
Hairpin lace or crocheted lace frame
Ruler
Scissors or pinking shears
Optional: hand-held twisting tool with cup hook in end

Instructions:

1. Cut the fabric to fit around the file (including the inner pocket), allowing an extra 1-1/4" to extend over all the ends.

2. Working one section at a time, spread a light covering of tacky glue over the front flap and top edge. Press the fabric in place, smoothing out any wrinkles or bubbles. Allow to dry. Repeat for the back and inside pocket front.

3. Fold in the raw fabric edges along the lower edge of the front flap and the inside pocket front and glue. Use paper clips to hold the raw edges in place while the glue dries.

4. Using the traditional folding method for wrapping packages, fold in one side edge of the fabric and glue. Let dry. Repeat on the other side edge.

Fringe, Tassel & Cord

1. To make the **fringe**, adjust the hairpin lace frame so there is a 2" span between the rods.

2. Holding one strand each of the three different yarns, make 56 wraps around the rods. Secure the ends.

3. Using a zipper foot, sew along one edge of the fringe, close to the rod. Slide the fringe off the frame. Repeat steps 2 and 3.

4. To make the **tassel**, adjust the Trim Tool to make a 3" long tassel. Holding the three strands of yarn together, make 40 wraps. Complete the tassel, following the Trim Tool instructions.

5. Thread the two charms with gold rayon crochet thread and affix them to the tassel, allowing them to hang down in front of the skirt.

6. To make the **cord**, hold the three strands of yarn together and wind off approximately three yards. Tie the ends together to form a circle.

7. Hang the end opposite the knot on a hook and use the twisting tool or a pencil inserted through the knotted end to twist the yarn until it kinks tightly when released.

8. Let the yarn double back on itself to create the cording. Remove from the hook, holding the end, and knot this end with the knotted end.

Embellishments

1. Cut a 6" length of cord and attach it to the top of the tassel. *Note: When cutting pieces of cord for the tassel, be sure to make two knots on each side of the cut first.*

2. To apply the fringe to the box, mark the center point of the flap's bottom edge and the two upper side edges of the flap. Draw straight lines between the marked points, creating a V (refer to the photo).

3. Apply a fine line of fabric glue along these lines and adhere the top sewn edge of the fringe, extending the fringe along the top side edges of the front flap. Secure with a heavy book until dry.

4. To apply the cording, apply a thin line of fabric glue along the machine stitching at the top of the fringe and adhere the cording. Secure with a heavy book until dry.

5. Draw two loops on the center top of the front flap, using the photo as guide. Apply fabric glue along these lines and adhere the cord attached to the tassel, letting the tassel hang down. (Be sure the side of the tassel with the charms faces out.)

The following products were used for this project: Rayon Chenille by Ruby Mills, Trim Tool by Susan Bates.

Cari's Intermediate Project

Tasseled Triples

The idea for this "box" came from my supply of cones accumulated during years of machine knitting, although you can purchase these cones at any craft store. Any gift that comes in threes (earrings, bracelet, necklace; trio of cosmetics or fragrances) is ideal, although it is suitable for nearly any small set of gifts. It can be hung with the Christmas stockings from the tree or from a doorknob as an extra special touch. Rather than making a lid, use gold tissue paper to cover the gifts.

Instructions:

1. Cut a piece of fabric to fit around a cone, allowing an extra 1" to extend over the wide end (top) of the cone and 1/2" over the narrow (bottom) end.

2. Apply a thick coating of spray adhesive on the cone and adhere the fabric around it, folding and overlapping the fabric at the join.

3. Clip the 1" fabric extension around the top at 1" intervals and fold the raw edges to the inside and glue. Secure with paper clips until the glue dries.

4. Push the 1/2" fabric extension at the bottom of the cone inside through the small hole.

5. Cut off any excess fabric at the join. (The raw edge doesn't need to be finished since it won't be visible when the three cones are connected.)

6. Repeat for two of the remaining cones (the fourth cone is used for the tassel finial).

7. Spread a thick line of tacky glue where the cones will meet, making sure the fabric joins are positioned facing the inside. Hold the cones together with rubber bands until the glue dries.

Three Hanging Cords

1. Holding one strand of each color floss together, wind off approximately four yards. Tie the ends together to form a circle.

2. Hang the end opposite the knot on a hook and use the twisting tool or a pencil inserted through the knotted end to twist the yarn until it kinks tightly when released.

3. Let the yarn double back on itself to create the cord. Remove it from the hook, holding the end and knot this end with the previously knotted end.

4. Cut an 18" length of cord for each cone. *Note: When cutting pieces of cord, be sure to make two knots on each side of the cut first.*

5. Use the awl or the point of the scissors to make a hole in the outer top edge of each cone (refer to the photo).

6. Thread the yarn darner with the cord and insert the cord from the outside to the inside so the knot holds the cord in place.

7. Bring all three cords together at the top and knot. Cut the ends above the knot to create a fringe effect.

Materials:

(4) 2-3/4" diameter corrugated cones (usually used for angel bodies)
1/4 yard each of three coordinating fabrics
2 skeins rayon embroidery floss
2 skeins cotton embroidery floss in contrasting color
1 card metallic gold yarn
Large-eyed gold disk bead
Spray adhesive
Tacky glue
Thick rubber bands
Tassel Magic tool (for creating bullion tassel skirt)
Awl or sharp pointed scissors
Paper clips
Ruler
Pencil
Tape
Coping saw or strong box knife
Yarn darner

Tassel

1. Set the Tassel Magic tool to make a 3" tassel.

2. Separate both the rayon and cotton floss skeins into three strands and wind them on a floss card.

3. Use the Tassel Magic tool to make bullion fringe across the full length of the joined boards, following the instructions for the tool.

4. Remove the fringe from the board and wind it on the straw that comes with the Tassel Magic, following the product instructions. Set aside.

5. To make the tassel top finial, measure and mark 1-1/2" from the tip of the unfinished cone. Use a coping saw or box knife to cut off this 1-1/2" tip.

6. Apply spray adhesive around the outside of the tip and wrap the finial with gold metallic yarn.

7. Cut three 12" lengths of cotton floss. Keeping the three strands together, wind them vertically on the finial, creating four triple strands (one in each quarter of the finial). Glue the ends inside the finial.

8. Cut one 12" length of rayon floss and wind as above, positioning the one rayon strand between the triple strands of cotton.

Cord & Tassel

1. Make a 24" cord (see Hanging Cord instructions above) for the tassel hanging cords.

2. Apply tape every 8" on the cord (to create three equal lengths). Cut in the center of the tape. Make a large knot at one end of each cord.

3. Using the yarn darner threaded with the cord, thread each cord through a different cone so the knot secures the cord at the tip of the cone.

4. Pick up the tassel skirt wrapped around the straw and the finial.

5. Working each cord separately, thread the end through the top of the finial, through the center of the tassel skirt, and through the straw.

6. Tie the three cords together in a large knot so the measurement between the cones and the finial is 2".

Note: Put a bit of fiberfill or cotton in the bottom of each cone before filling them.

The following products were used for this project: Tassel Magic by CC Product Co./Bond America.

Bolster Pillow Box

Cari's
Advanced
Project

This "box" is designed to imitate a bolster pillow and can be a gift in and of itself. However, it will house any long or soft gift: wooded knitting needles and fancy yarn, gloves and scarf, a rolled poster, etc. Note: Remove the end caps by pulling on the edges of the caps rather than just the tassel. You can also use this design idea for making a shorter "bolster" from an oatmeal container, with only one end opening.

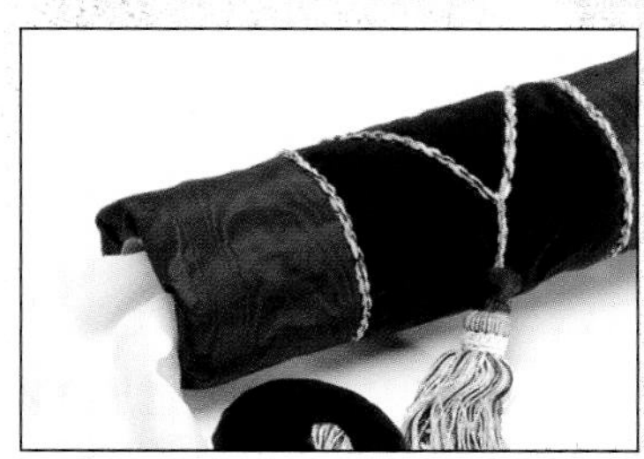

Materials:

3" diameter mailing tube, cut to 15" long
1/2 yard quilt batting
1/4 yard hunter green velveteen
1/4 yard matching green moiré
Sheet 1/4" foam board
Sewing thread to match fabric
2 florist stem wires
1" wood cabinet knob
(2) 1" doll pin stands
3/4" wood wheel
(2) 1/2" long large-holed cylindrical wood beads
3 skeins hunter green perle 5 cotton
3 skeins camel perle 5 cotton
1 spool Multi's Embellishment Yarn, color Antique
6" ecru decorative trim, 1/2"-wide
Drill with 1/8" drill bit
Coping saw or strong box knife
Spray adhesive
Fabric glue
Tacky glue
Tassel Magic tool, Tatool, or hairpin lace frame

Instructions:

Tube

1. Cut the batting to 15" wide.

2. Remove the caps on the mailing tube and spray a film of adhesive around the outside of the tube. Wrap the batting twice around the tube. Cut off the excess and baste the join to the first layer, making sure the batting doesn't extend beyond the ends of the tube.

3. Cut one 8" x 14" piece of velveteen and two 7" x 14" pieces of moiré.

4. Sew one moiré piece on each 14" side of the velveteen, using a 1/2" seam. Fold the long edges under 1/2" and press to the wrong side.

5. Wrap this around the batting (approximately 1" will extend off each end) and slipstitch in place.

6. Clip the extra fabric on the ends at 1" intervals and fold to the inside of the tube. Secure with tacky glue.

End Caps

1. Cut two 4" diameter foam board circles. Make two small holes 1/8" apart in the center of the circles.

2. Cut two 8" diameter circles from the velveteen and batting. Using long basting stitches and a double strand of thread, sew the batting and velveteen together 1/2" from the edges. Don't knot or break off the thread.

3. Position the foam board circle in the center of the velveteen. Pull the thread ends to gather the edges of the velveteen circle so it encloses the foam board circle. Tie the thread ends together to secure. Repeat for the other end cap.

Hanging Cords

1. Make one 30" long cord and one 20" long cord by measuring off 5 yards for the longer cord and 3-1/2 yards for the shorter cord of each of the following: 1 strand green perle cotton, 1 strand camel perle cotton, and 1 strand Multi's.

2. Tie the 5-yard length of the three strands together to form a circle.

3. Divide this in half and loop the end opposite the knot on a hook or doorknob. Insert a pencil in the knotted end and twist clockwise until the cord is relatively tight. Hang a weight on the cording, unhook the cording, and bring the ends together, being sure to keep a firm hold on both ends. Knot the ends.

4. Remove the weight and let the cording twist back on itself. This piece will be used to embellish the pillow.

5. Repeat with the 3-1/2-yard length to make the 24" cord.

6. Cut the 24" cord into two 6" lengths and one 12" length, each separated by two knots. Cut between the knots so there are two short and one long length of cord.

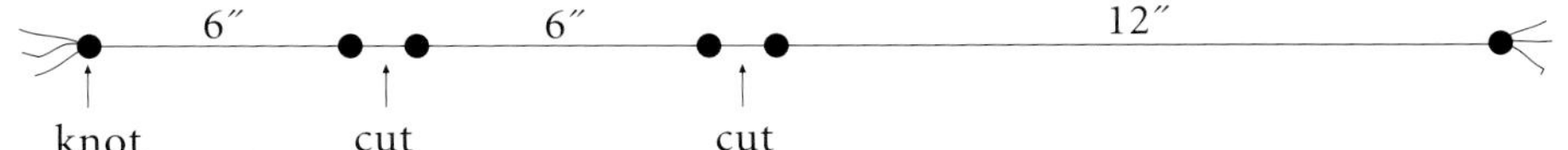

Large Tassel

Doll pin stands.

1. Using a 1/8" bit, drill a hole in the cabinet knob.

2. Wrap a doll pin stand (through the hole) with one strand green perle cotton and one strand Multi's.

3. Glue the ecru trim around the second doll pin stand.

4. Glue the wider sections of the two doll pin stands together.

5. Glue the cabinet knob to the narrow end of the yarn-wrapped doll pin stand.

6. Apply a layer of spray adhesive on the outside of the cabinet knob and wrap it with green perle cotton.

7. To make the tassel skirt, use one of the tassel tools or a hairpin lace frame set for a 4" tassel skirt or fringe. Wrap one strand each of the two perle cottons and Multi's around the frame so there is a 9" length of fringe. Secure along the top of the fringe by sewing or taping. Follow the directions for the tassel tool to make the 4" tassel.

8. Thread the 12" cord through the wood wheel, using the knot as a stop. Thread the cord through the bottom of the tassel, coming out the top of the finial. You will use this cord to attach the tassel to the pillow later.

Two Small Tassels

1. Make a skirt using a tassel tool set for 3" long and 6" wide.

2. Glue a piece of ecru trim around each of the two cylindrical wooden beads.

3. Wrap green floss around the top of the tassel, just above the trimmed bead.

4. Make the tassel skirt, following the tassel tool instructions.

5. Make a large knot in the 6" cord and draw it through the bottom of the tassel skirt and the wooden bead to form a small loop. This loop will allow you to attach the tassel to the end caps.

Finishing

1. Hand stitch the 30" cord on top of one seam around the pillow, attaching it at the join. Bring the cord to the center of the velveteen section. Catch the hanging cord of the tassel and repeat for the opposite side of the pillow, reversing the application of the cording.

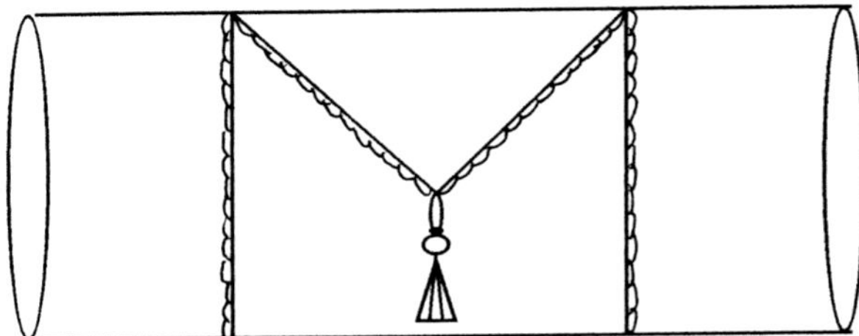

2. Make two 1/8" holes in the center of the plastic end caps for the mailing tube.

3. Fold one of the stem wires in half and insert one end into the fabric, through one hole in the foam board, and through the corresponding hole in the end cap.

4. Thread the second half of the stem wire through the looped hanging cord at the top of one of the small tassels. Insert the stem wire back into the fabric, foam board, and end cap and twist the two halves together on the inside. Cut off the remaining wire and bend it toward the end cap. Repeat for the other end cap.

The following products were used for this project: Multi's Embellishment Thread, Tassel Magic by CC Product Co./Bond America, or Tatool by On the Surface.

Back Seat Travel Checkerboard

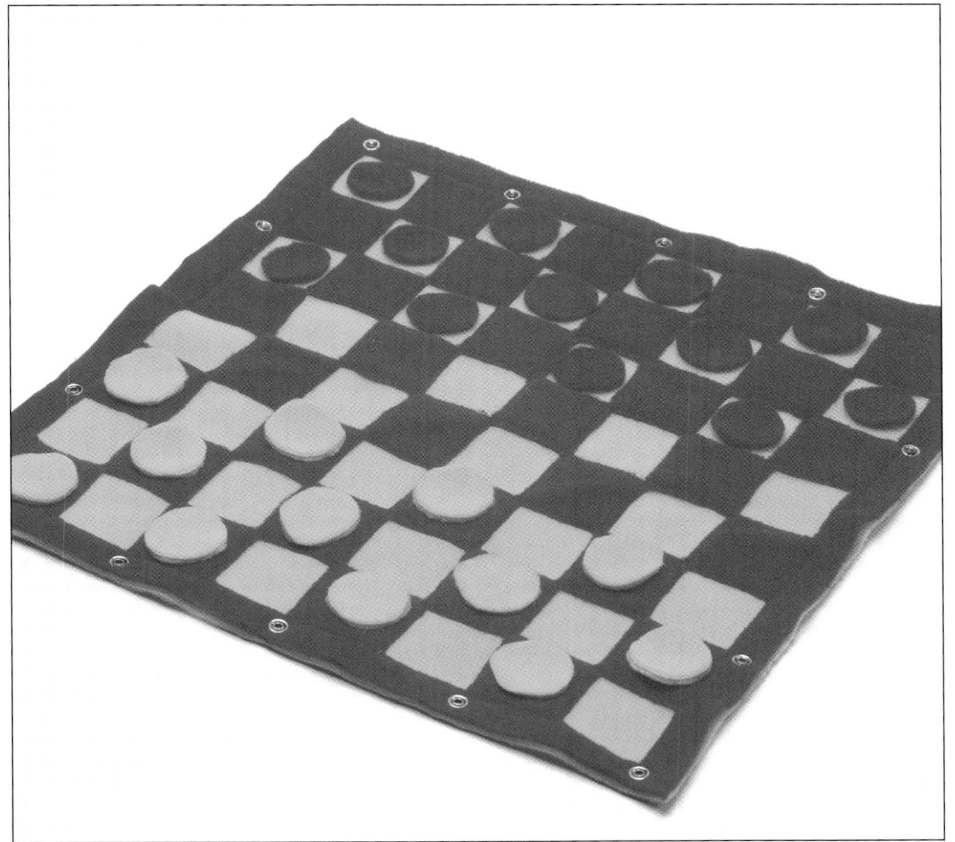

This idea offers a different interpretation to the "Treasured Wrappings" theme. The "wrapping" is the checkerboard itself, since it snaps closed to hold the checkers inside. Roll and tie, or store folded and flat, depending on how much car space is available. It is a "treasured" gift because it keeps little travelers occupied, providing "treasured" peace and quiet for the parents. A great gift for any family that takes long car trips.

Choose bright colors. Strong colors help to hold the children's interest, while being easy to find if pieces fall on the car floor.

The nap of the fleece holds the checkers in place. No slipping and sliding with the jostling of the car!

Nancy's Beginner Project

Nancy Cornwell

Nancy is affectionately known as the "Polar Princess" following the success of her books, Adventures With Polarfleece® *and* More Polarfleece® Adventures. *She has been an avid sewer and designer since her teens. Nancy's sewing philosophy is to make it fast, fun, and easy. Her ideas for this book fit that philosophy perfectly.*

Materials:

Two solid colors fleece, mid to heavier weight, 18" x 24" of each
Regular thread to match both fleece colors
7 sport snaps, size 20
18" cord for tie
Rotary cutter and mat
Small sharp scissors

Instructions:

1. Cut 18" x 18" squares from both fleeces.

2. Place the fleeces wrong sides together. Pin to hold, placing the pins at a 90° angle to the cut edges.

3. With matching threads in the needle and bobbin and using a conventional sewing machine, sew around all four sides with a 1" seam allowance.

4. Using a rotary cutter and ruler, slightly trim the outer edges to neaten.

5. Attach a quilt bar (spacer bar, edge guide) to your machine and straight stitch the checkerboard squares by sewing 2" horizontal and vertical rows between the outer seamlines.

6. Using sharp scissors, trim just the top layer from every other square to reveal the contrast color fleece underneath. Trim close to the stitching lines.

7. Using the excess fleece from step #1, cut 1-1/2" circles from each fleece color for the checker pieces. Sixteen pieces are needed for the game. Cut and save extra pieces in case some get lost. (An easy way to cut the circles is to first cut 2" squares, then trim the edges away, rounding the corners.)

8. Evenly space five sport snaps along two opposite sides of the checkerboard. Place the remaining two snaps, one on each side edge, at the end of the second row of squares.

9. To store, place the checker pieces on the board, fold the board in half, and snap to secure. Roll up and tie or store flat, depending on car storage space.

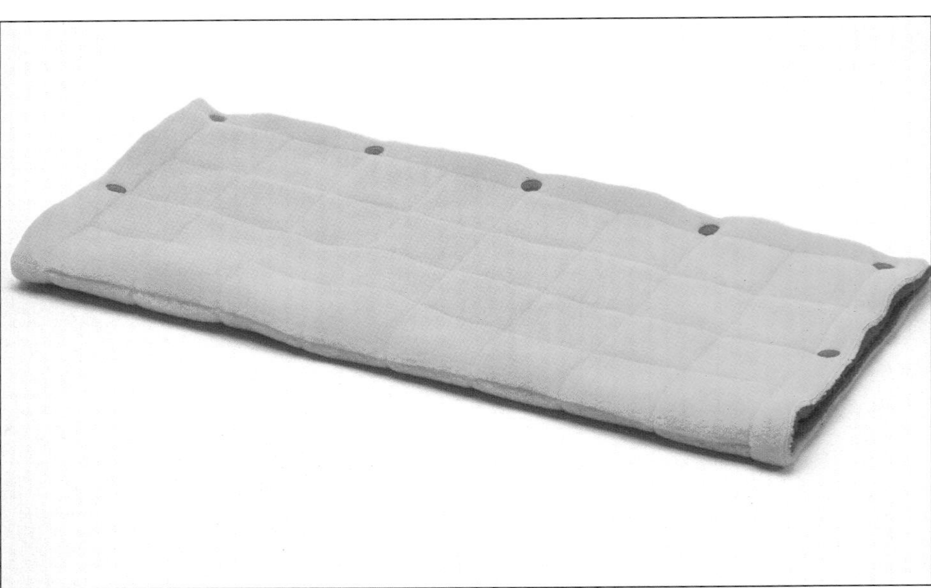

Wine Cooler

Nancy's Intermediate Project

Sew this clever gift wine bag to make your housewarming bottle of wine or congratulatory bottle of champagne just a little more special. Use the thermal qualities of Polarfleece® "in reverse." Instead of using the fleece to keep warm, use the insulation qualities to keep a gift bottle of chilled wine cool!

Choose a splashy cotton print for the outside layer and fleece for the liner. Choose the print according to the occasion (balloon and ribbon print for a birthday, home dec print for housewarming, metallic print for congratulations, heart print for Valentine's or romance, etc.). Depending on how fancy you want to get (or how expensive the wine is), you can tie the gift bag with a dramatic upholstery cord and tassels, decorative gold braid, a narrow strip of UltraSuede, wire-edged ribbon, or simple gift ribbon.

Your personally made Wine Cooler is a nice (and easy) way to dress up your "tasteful" gift.

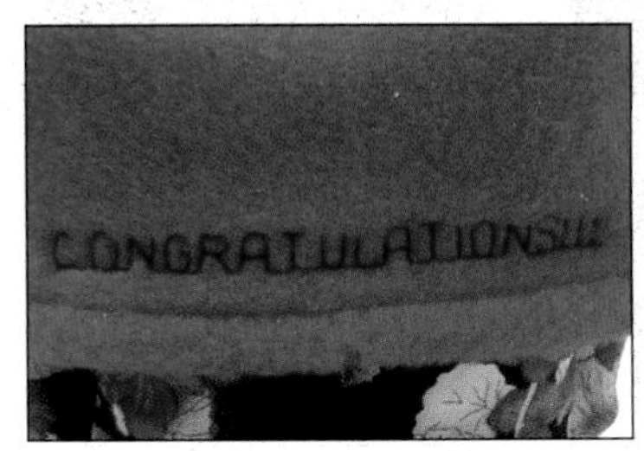

Materials:

Woven cotton print, 15" x 20"
Solid color fleece, 15" x 20"
Thread
Decorative thread (for lettering your message)
1 yard ribbon, cord, or braid for tie

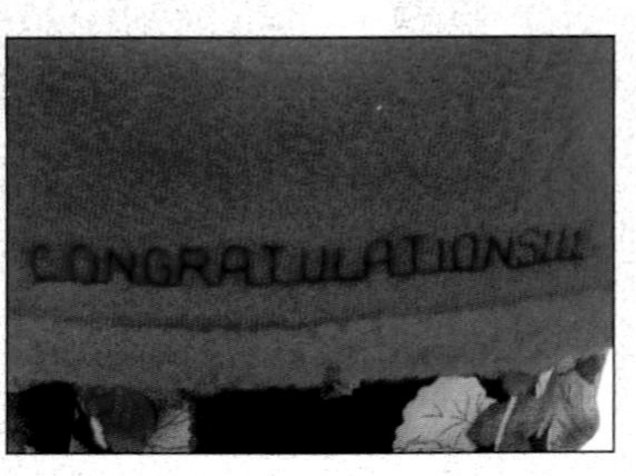

Instructions:

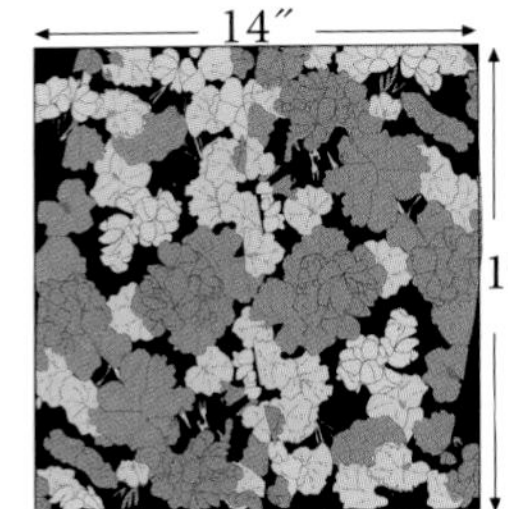

Sew with 1/4" seam allowance.

1. Cut one each from solid fleece and print fabric: 4-1/2" diameter circle for the base; 15" x 14" rectangle for the sides

2. With wrong sides together, baste the fleece and print fabric circles together along the outer edges.

3. Fold the fleece side section in half (15" x 7") with right sides together and sew to form a tube. Repeat for the print fabric side section. Turn the print fabric tube right side out.

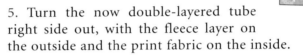

4. With right sides together, insert the print fabric tube into the fleece tube, matching the raw edges at one end. Stitch that end.

5. Turn the now double-layered tube right side out, with the fleece layer on the outside and the print fabric on the inside.

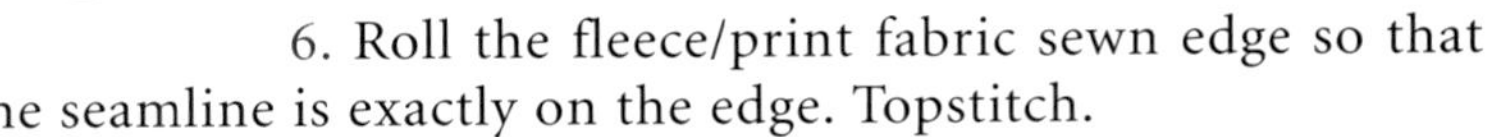

6. Roll the fleece/print fabric sewn edge so that the seamline is exactly on the edge. Topstitch.

7. Matching the raw edges, sew the wine cooler sack bottom (basted circles) to the other end of the tube with the print fabric facing the inside of the tube (both the fleece tube and the fleece circle are facing out).

8. Turn the wine cooler sack to the finished position (print fabric out). Using decorative thread, machine stitch an appropriate message above the topstitching line on the fleece side of the sack (Congratulations! Happy Birthday! Good Luck! Well Done! Best Wishes!).

9. Mark the midpoint of a 30" piece of ribbon or decorative cord. Sew the cord/ribbon midpoint to the tube seam 4-1/2" below the topstitched open end.

10. Insert a chilled bottle of wine and tie. Turn back the cuff to reveal the message on the fleece liner and expose the bottle top.

Flower Pot Reversible Pantaloons

Nancy's Advanced Project

Enjoy giving potted plants and flowers as gifts but want to add your personal touch to the gift? Dress up a plain flower pot with pretty pantaloons. Since the pantaloons are reversible, choose one print to reflect the "special occasion."

Possible print themes include birthday, spring, summer, autumn, winter, Valentine's Day, St. Patrick's Day, Easter, Fourth of July, Halloween, Thanksgiving, Christmas, etc. Choose the print colors to complement each other, since hints of the reverse side will be visible at the ruffled edge.

Materials:

to hold a 6" pot

5/8 yard each of two complementary woven cotton prints (enough to dress two pots)
2 yards 1"-wide white ruffled lace
2 yards double-sided, picot-edged 1/2"-wide ribbon
Bodkin
Thread to match both fabric layers

Instructions:

1. To draw the pantaloon pattern piece, trace a circle around the base of the flower pot, then measure the height of the flower pot and enlarge the circle by this measurement. Enlarge the circle an additional 2" for the ruffle.

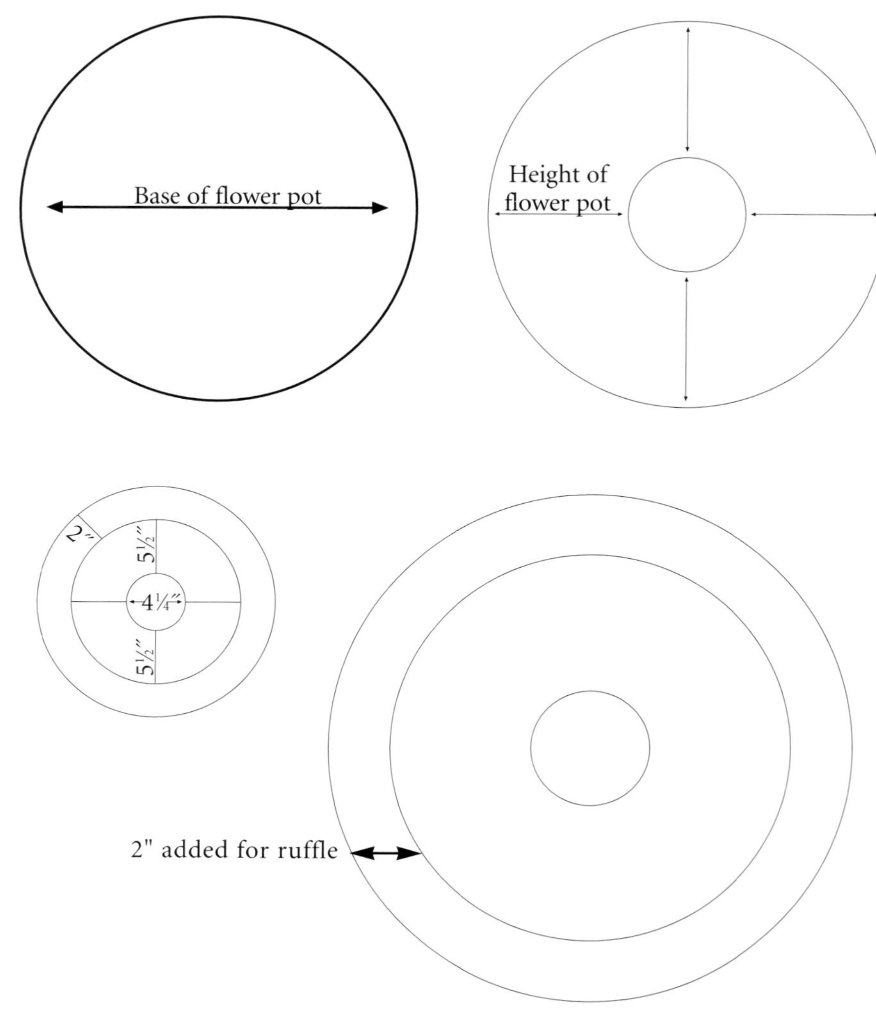

2. Cut out a circle from both prints.

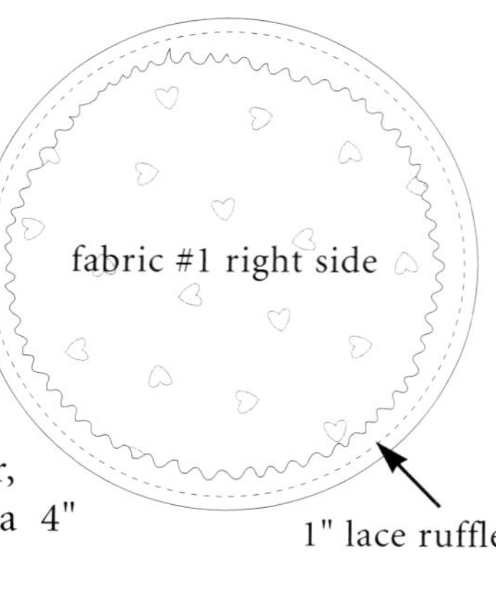

3. Sew lace to the right side of one circle with a 1/4" seam allowance, keeping the outer edges even. Overlap the beginning and end of the lace 1".

4. Pin the print circles right sides together, sandwiching the lace. Sew the circles together, following the previous stitching line. Leave a 4" opening to turn.

5. Turn the circles right sides out, hand stitch the opening, and press.

6. To mark placement for the buttonholes, fold the circles in half and pin mark the halves.

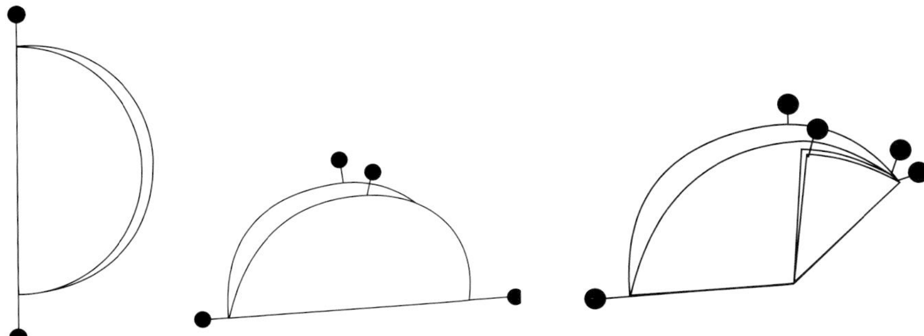

Fold the circles in half the other way, matching the pinned half marks, and pin mark the quarter marks.

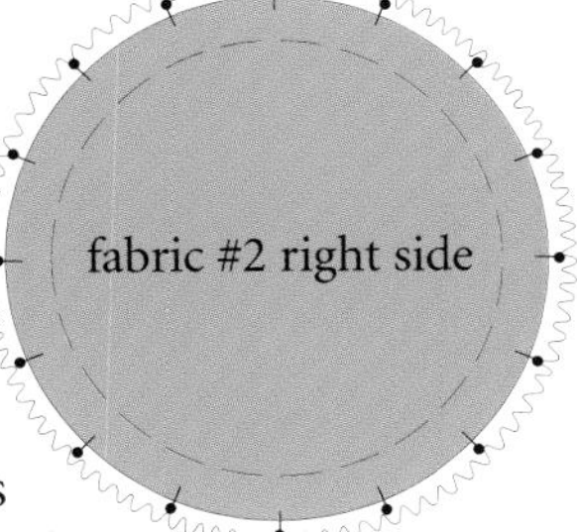

Fold the circles again, matching the quarter marks, and pin mark eighths.

Fold the circles again, matching the eighth marks and pin mark sixteenths. At each sixteenth pin mark, draw a line for buttonholes 1-1/2" away from the seamed edge.

7. Sew pairs of 5/8" buttonholes 1/2" apart, beginning at the marked lines. (Place different colored thread in the needle and bobbin to match the differing fabrics.)

8. Using a bodkin, pull the ribbon through the buttonholes, weaving the ribbon under the fabric between the closely spaced buttonholes and over the fabric at the wider spaces.

9. Place the flower pot in the center of the circle, tie the ribbon to gather the edges. Arrange the gathers and ruffle.

weave ribbon in and out of buttonholes

Lynne's Beginner Project

Lynne Farris

Lynne brings a fresh approach and limitless creative energy to every challenge. She was selected as one of five Craft Designers of the Year in 1994 and appears frequently in print, on television, and at seminars and trade shows.

Just for Kids: My Very Own Keepsake Box

Delight a special child with a keepsake gift box designed just for them. This easy to make beginner project features a purchased fabric-covered box embellished with soft sculpted flowers in primary colors. Matching tubular fabric cording creates the look of frosting on the cake!

Instructions:

1. Fold the flower and leaf fabrics in double thickness with right sides together. Trace the flower and leaf patterns on the wrong side of the fabric. *Before cutting out*, sew around the traced lines.

2. Cut out three flowers and two leaves, leaving 1/4" seam allowances. Cut a small slit in the center of one side of each of the flowers and leaves for turning.

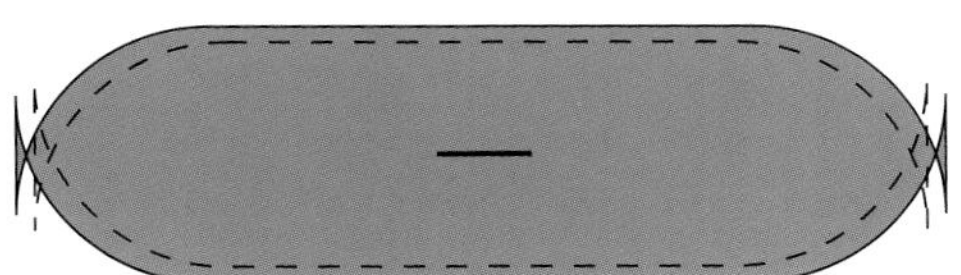

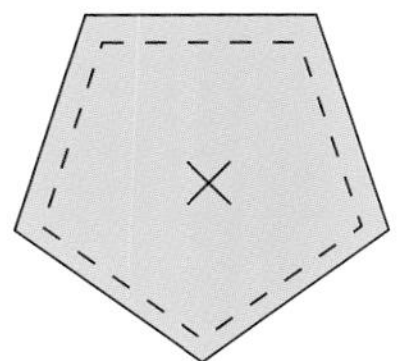

3. Turn right side out through the slit and hand stitch the slit closed. Attach a button to the center of the flowers. Pinch the leaves together at the center to create a pleat and hand stitch to secure.

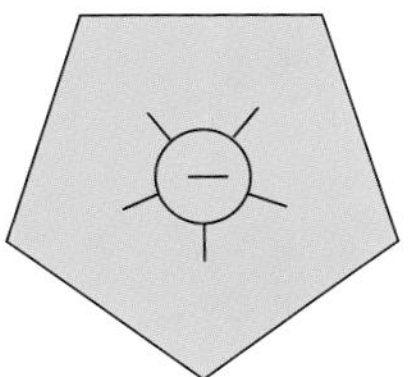

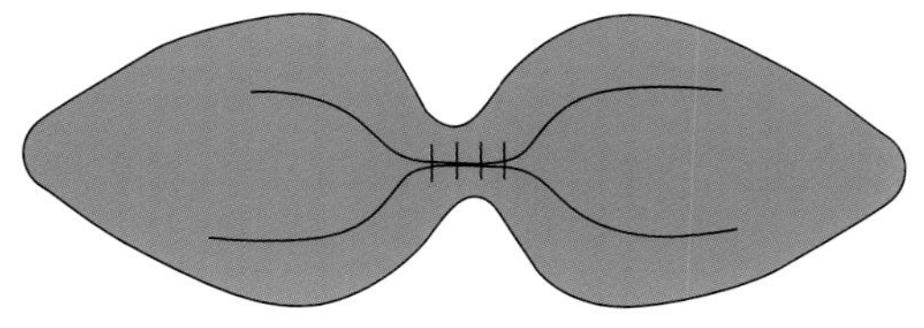

4. Using the photo as a guide, arrange the leaves and flowers on top of the box to form a bouquet and glue in place.

5. To make the cording, measure around the lid and add 1". Cut two fabric strips this length and 2" wide. Fold in half lengthwise and sew 1/4" from the cut edge. Close one end by stitching across. Turn right side out, using a skewer or turning tool.

6. With the seam to the inside, glue the cording around the lid and the lower edge of the box.

The following products were used for this project: Prym Dritz Muslin-Covered Oval Box, Crafter's Pick Ultimate Tacky Adhesive (API).

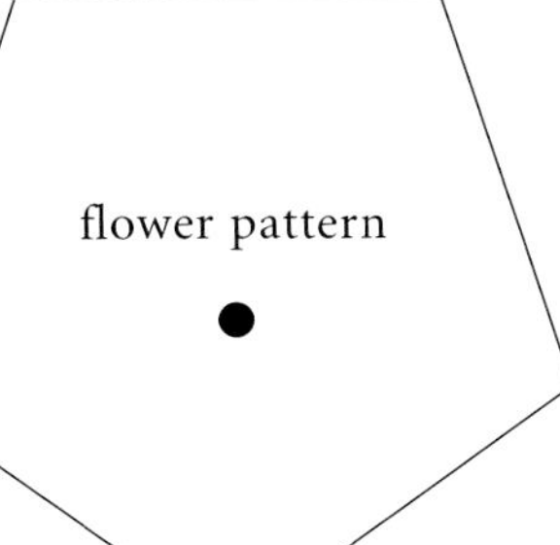

Materials:

Muslin-covered oval box
Small scraps (at least 6" x 6") colorful knit fabric such as sweatshirt fleece, fleece, or velour in red, yellow, and blue
1/8 yard green knit fabric for leaves and cording
3 green buttons for flower centers, 1/4" diameter
Matching thread
Tacky adhesive or glue gun
Air-soluble marker

Lynne's Intermediate Project

Gifts for Guys: Leopard Print Velvet Gift Bag

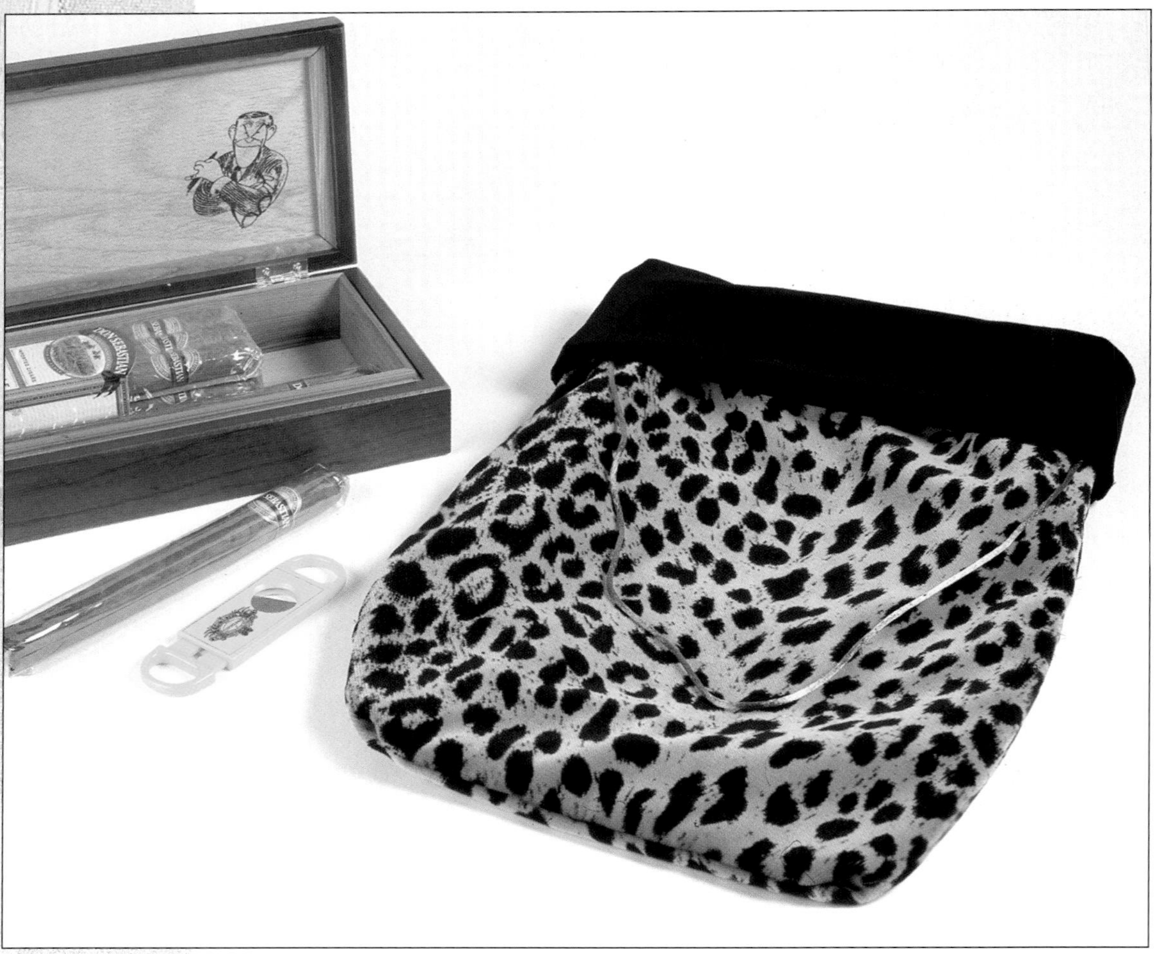

This attractive reusable gift pouch is an easy way to wrap an odd-shaped gift such as a small gadget or even a group of small items. It's sure to impress the man in your life. The leopard print velvet with a contrasting black velvet cuff and lining lends a masculine touch. A coordinating cord tie keeps the gift under wraps.

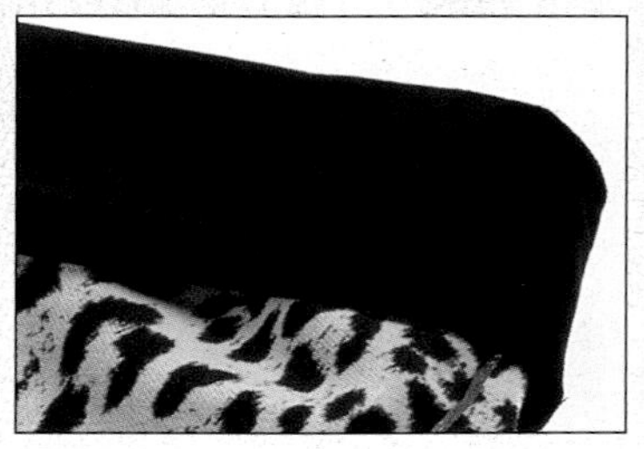

Instructions:

1. Place the two pieces of print velvet right sides together. Using a jar lid or other 3" to 4" circle as a guide, mark curves at the two bottom corners. Sew down one side, along the bottom, and up the other side. Leave the top open.

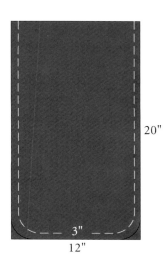

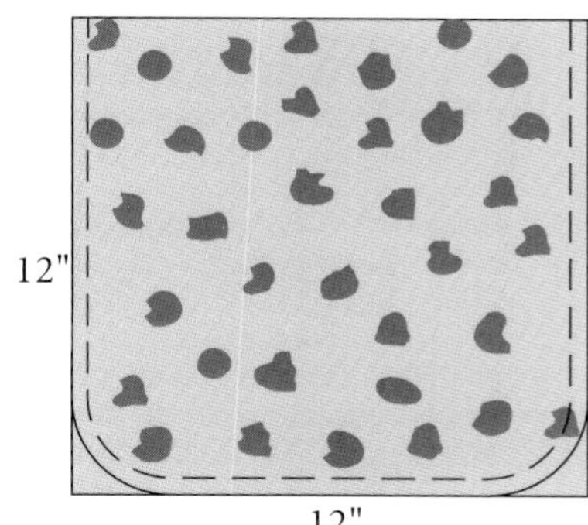

2. Repeat the process with the black velvet, except leave a 3" gap in the center of the seam between the curved corners for turning. You'll end up with a rectangle approximately 12" x 20".

3. With right sides together, place the print bag inside the black bag, matching the seams. Insert the ends of the cord at the side seam and sew around the upper edge.

4. Turn right side out through the opening in the black bag. Hand stitch the opening. Fold back the excess length of black velvet to form a contrasting cuff.

Materials:

2 pieces 12" x 12" leopard print velvet
2 pieces 12" x 20" black velvet
1 yard tan rattail cording
Coordinating thread
Scissors
Marking pen
Note: This bag can be sized for any odd-shaped gift. Just adjust the fabric measurements as needed.

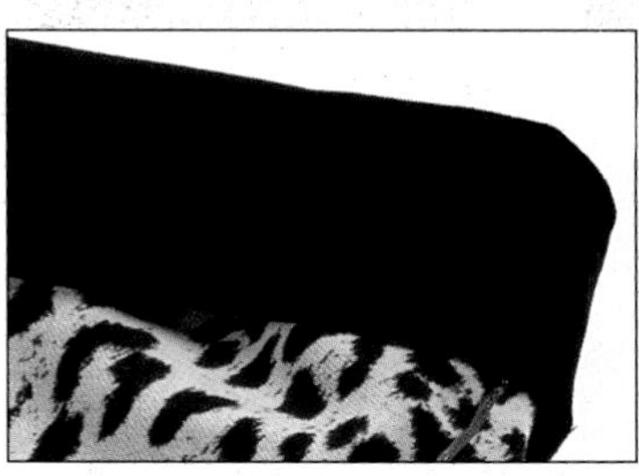

Lynne's Advanced Project

Elegant Woven Ribbon Keepsake Bag

This luxurious woven ribbon keepsake bag holds the promise of a very special gift indeed. You can choose rich and royal jewel tones as I did, or coordinate soft pastels for a elegant bridal or graduation gift. In any case, your gift is sure to create lasting memories.

Instructions:

1. Place the fusible tricot on the ironing board with the adhesive facing up.

2. Arrange the 18" ribbon strips of various colors and widths lengthwise with the edges touching one another to cover the fusible tricot (I used 13 strips). Pin the ribbons in place on the ironing board to secure.

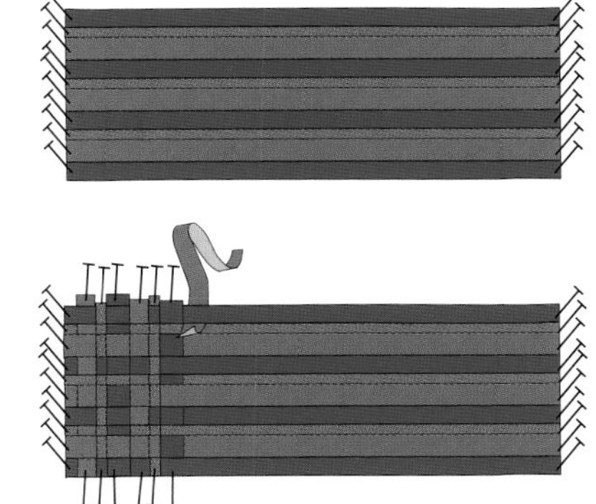

3. Cut the remaining ribbons in half and weave these 9" strips between the 18" strips to form solidly woven ribbon fabric. Pin the ends in place to secure.

4. Place a press cloth over the entire surface and press, following the manufacturer's instructions for the fusible tricot to adhere the ribbon strips to the tricot.

5. Remove the pins. Fold the woven ribbon fabric in half with the right sides together and sew around the sides and bottom to form a bag, using a 1/2" seam allowance. Trim to 1/4" or clean finish the seam allowances with serged edges or seam tape.

6. Fold the wire edged taffeta ribbon in half lengthwise and sew a double row of basting stitches near the fold. Pull the lower threads to gather, forming a ruffle to fit around the top of the bag. Sew the ends together, then pin it in place around the bag, matching the seams. Sew in place. Turn the gathered edge to the inside of the bag and stitch to conceal the rough seam allowances.

7. To form the drawstring, tie knots at the ends of the cord and thread it through the loose ribbons around the upper edge of the bag just below the ruffle. Tie in a pretty bow.

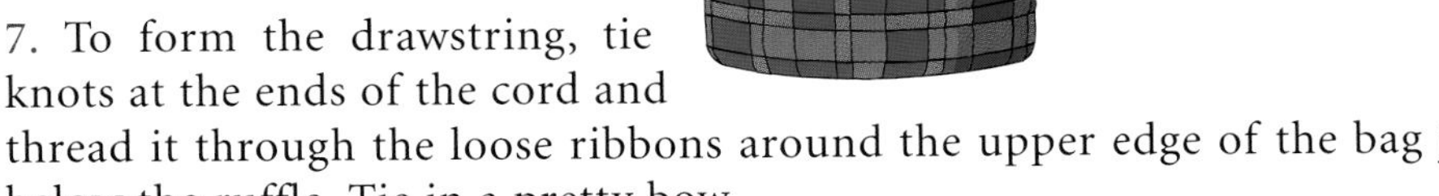

The following products were used for this project: Fusible Tricot Lining by Handler Textiles, Offray Ribbons.

Materials:

7" x 18" piece fusible tricot lining
(20) 18" pieces single face satin and velvet ribbons in coordinating colors and varying widths from 1/4" to 1" (more if you use narrower ribbons)
1 yard wire edged taffeta ribbon, 5"-wide
1 yard cord, 1/2"-diameter
Iron
Press cloth
Scissors

Emi's Beginner Project

Emi Fukushima

Emi's specialty is washi paper, although she also works with polymer clay and painting. She travels worldwide teaching and demonstrating arts and crafts.

Washi or Origami Paper Gift Bag

This bag is so easy to make, you'll want to keep several on hand for last minute gift giving occasions.

Washi Paper

Washi (Japanese handmade paper) is remarkable for its combination of lightness, strength, and flexibility. Traditionally, this paper was used for writing, calligraphy, bookmaking, and for fans, umbrellas, masks, kites, clothing, and even windows.

Origami Paper

The Japanese word origami comes from the words ori (to fold) and kami or gami (paper). This art originated in Japan some 1400 years ago and can be defined as the art of manipulating a square of paper without cutting, pasting, decorating, or mutilating it in any way. It can only be folded.

The thin paper from Japan is brightly colored on one side and white on the reverse.

Note: If you are unable to find washi or origami paper, you can use gift wrap, wall-paper, or any decorative paper that's printed on only one side.

Materials:

to make a bag
6-1/2" x 3-3/4" x 2-1/4"

8-1/2" x 14" washi/origami paper
15-20 assorted beads
Decorative cord to match paper
Tacky glue
Paper edgers
Scissors
Hole punch
Pencil
Stylus
Ruler
Brush for glue

Instructions:

1. Carefully take apart a small lunch bag or other bag that's the size you want to make. Trace the bag pattern with a pencil on the back of the washi/origami paper and cut it out. (You can also use the pattern on page 112.)

2. Mark the fold lines on the washi/origami paper. Score the fold lines with a stylus.

3. Fold and crease along the scored lines and glue the washi/origami paper together to form a bag.

4. Fold the top opening of the bag together and cut evenly with the paper edgers.

5. Punch holes for the decorative cord.

6. Thread the cord with beads and knot the ends.

The following products were used for this project: Washi/Origami Paper by Aitoh Co., Beads by The Beadery, Gold Cord by Kreinik, Fiskars Paper Edgers, Delta Quik 'n Tacky Glue.

Emi's Intermediate Project

Washi or Origami Paper Boxes

Box stencils from American Traditional Stencils take the guesswork out of assembling these lovely boxes. The paper and ribbon make them extra special.

Instructions:

1. Trace the box pattern with a pencil on the plain art paper and cut out. Trace it again with a pencil on the back of the washi/origami paper and cut out.

2. Glue the two papers together with the design on the outside.

3. Score the fold lines with a stylus.

4. Fold and crease along the scored lines.

5. Assemble the box and glue it together.

6. Embellish with buttons, charms, tassels, or ribbon as desired.

The following products were used for this project: Washi/Origami Paper by Aitoh Co., Blue Laser Stencils by American Traditional - #BL-452 Large Cube (provided), #BL-449 Small Boxes, #BL-450 Pillow Box, #BL-448 Hexagonal Box, Charms from Boutique Trims, Offray Ribbon, Delta Archival Quality Glue.

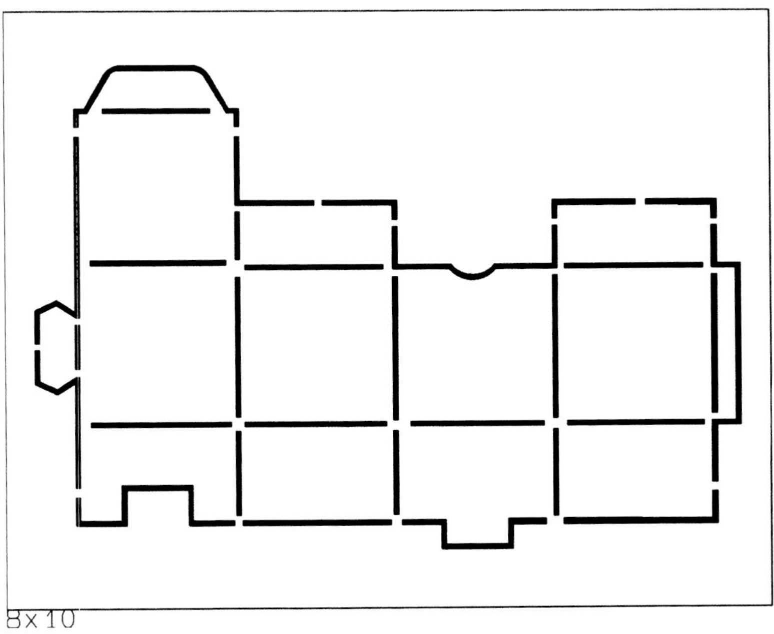

Enlarge 200%
Pattern courtesy of American Traditional Stencils

Materials:

8" x 10" washi/origami paper for each box
8" x 10" art paper for each box
Assorted ribbons, charms, buttons, tassels as desired
Archival quality glue
Stylus
Ruler
Brush for glue

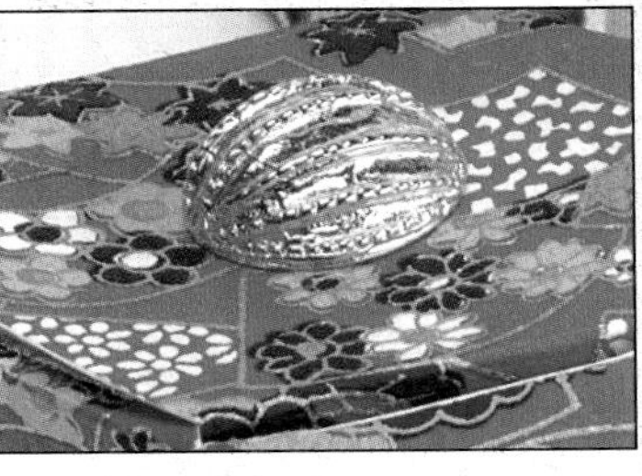

Emi's Advanced Project

Washi or Origami Paper Maché Gift Boxes

The lowly paper maché box is transformed by washi/origami paper and special embellishments.

Instructions:

1. Paint the inside of the paper maché box and lid.

2. Cut the washi/origami paper to cover the outside of the box (lid and bottom).

3. Use the archival quality glue to glue the paper to the box. Let dry completely.

4. Varnish or glaze the box and lid, inside and out.

5. Embellish the box with trims and charms, using tacky glue.

The following products were used for this project: Washi/Origami Paper by Aitoh Co., Kel-Toy Paper Maché Boxes, Delta Ceramcoat Acrylic Paint, Delta Archival Quality Glue, Delta Quik 'n Tacky Glue, Charms by Boutique Trims, Trims by Wrights.

Materials:

(2) 6" squares washi/origami paper for each box
3" x 4" paper maché box (rectangular or oval)
Acrylic paint to match paper
Assorted trims and charms
Scissors
Archival quality glue
Tacky glue
Varnish or glaze
Brush for glaze and glue

The Bride's Gift Box

Helen's Beginner Project

Helen Gibb

Helen is a native of Australia, now living in Colorado. Her design work includes ribbon art, decorative painting, rubber stamps, silk flower arrangements, and children's kits. Her book, The Secrets of Fashioning Ribbon Flowers, *offers making techniques and unique ways to decorate with ribbon flowers.*

This charming half-doll box makes a stunning wrapping! With the half-doll on the lid and the box forming the skirt, it is reminiscent of the vanity boxes found on a lady's boudoir table during the 1920s to store and cover utilitarian items. After removing the gift from this wonderful box, use the container for cotton balls, potpourri, hair pins or . . . lavender! Divide the tulle into small squares so it can hold lavender for your linen closet.

Instructions:

1. Glue the half-doll to the box lid, removing the button on the lid if necessary. Let dry.

2. Lightly glue pink/green ribbon braid around the half-doll's waist and glue a small piece to her hair. Glue the braid around the base of the box with tacky glue.

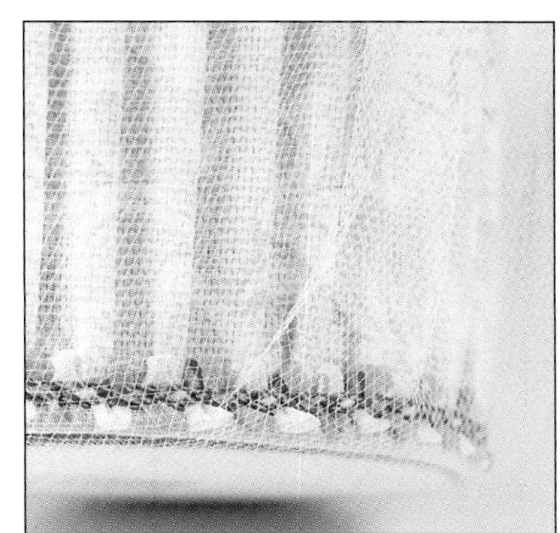

3. Place a bag of lavender inside the box.

4. Position the box in the center of the tulle square and draw up the edges. Tie with a simple shoelace bow around the half-doll's shoulders.

5. Arrange the tulle so the doll's face shows.

The following products were used for this project: Prym-Dritz St Jane Collection Box, Mokuba Ribbon, Porcelain Half Doll, Springwood Companies..

Materials:

Small fabric-covered round box
Porcelain half-doll (antique or reproduction)
20" square off-white tulle
1 yard off-white ribbon, 1"-wide
1/2 yard Mokuba pink and green ribbon braid
Dried lavender
E6000 glue
Tacky glue
Scissors

Helen's Intermediate Project

The Gardener's Gift Box

Trim a paper maché box and its rusty tin lid with French ribbons and a ribbon pansy. Add a few "tools" and you have the perfect gift presentation for the gardener. The box could hold a gift of gardening gloves and some seed packets. Make the pansy decoration removable and it can be used as a brooch or pinned on a garden hat.

Instructions:

1. Glue an 18" piece of brown/gold ribbon around the base of the box and a 10" piece across the top of the tin lid.

2. Tie a shoelace bow with 20" of the brown ribbon around two of the tool ornaments and glue it to the lid.

3. Tie another shoelace bow with 20" of the brown ribbon and stitch it to a 2" square of crinoline or felt.

4. Cut three 4" lengths of green ribbon and make three leaves by folding both ends of the ribbon down as shown. Stitch across the base of the triangle and gather very tightly and secure. Trim the tails.

5. Glue the leaves on top of the bow and crinoline.

6. Cut one 6-1/4" length and one 10-1/4" length of purple ribbon for the pansy.

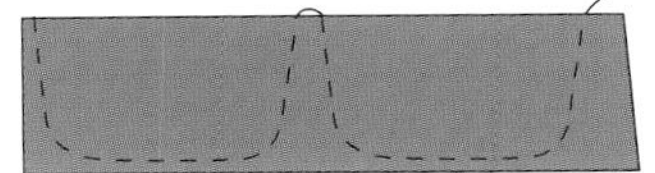

a. To make the back two petals, remove the wire from the gathering edge of the 6-1/4" piece of ribbon and mark the halfway point with a crease. Stitch the ribbon with a running stitch, leaving 1/8" margin at each raw edge. Tightly gather the ribbon and secure it when all is gathered. Attach these back petals to a 1" circle of crinoline near the gathered edge. Set aside.

b. To make the three front petals, remove the wire from the gathering edge of the 10-1/4" ribbon. Crease the ribbon in three sections, measuring from left to right, 3-1/8", 4", and 3-1/8". Stitch with a running stitch. Gather tightly and secure the gathering. Join the first petal to the last petal at the center.

c. To make the pansy center, make a plain overhand knot in the 3" piece of narrow yellow ribbon. Push the knot through the pansy center. Place the front petals on top of and slightly below the two back petals on the crinoline so the back petals peek out. Stitch in place. Trim the excess crinoline.

7. Glue the pansy on top of the leaves, bow, and crinoline.

8. Glue the pitchfork under the pansy. Trim the excess crinoline or felt from the arrangement.

9. Glue or stitch a pinback on the pansy composition and pin it to the top of the lid over the other bow and tools.

The following products were used for this project: Westrim Paper Maché Box with Tin Lid, Westrim Tool Ornaments, Ribbons by The Ribbon Club.

Materials:

5-3/4" round paper maché box with rusty tin lid
28" brown and gold ribbon, 1-1/2"-wide
40" brown wired ribbon, 1"-wide
18" purple/plum wired ribbon, 1"-wide
3" yellow silk embroidery ribbon, 7mm
1/3 yard green wired ribbon, 1-1/2"-wide
3" square crinoline or felt
Set of rusty tin "tools" ornaments
1" long pinback
Hot glue gun
Scissors
Needle and thread

Helen's Advanced Project

The Rose Gift Bag

Make a luxurious gift bag from floral fabric and trim it with silk ribbon roses and ribbons. When the gift has been removed, use the bag as a book tote, a fancy shopping bag, a lingerie bag, or hang it on a peg for a decorative accent. You could even make a pillow out of the bag by removing the handles, filling the bag with batting, and stitching the closure shut.

Instructions:

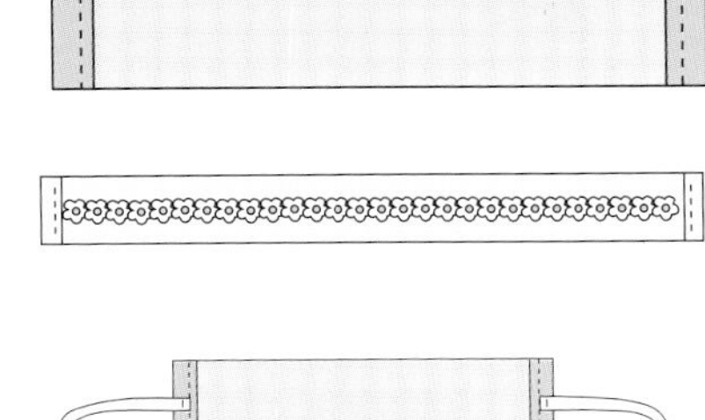

1. Stitch 1/2" hems on each 13" end of the bag fabric.

2. Cut the cream striped ribbon in two 17" lengths for the handles. Turn up the raw edges 1/2" and before hemming, tack a piece of cream flower trim to each handle.

3. Sew the handle to the inside edges of the bag.

4. With right sides of the fabric together and a 1/2" seam allowance, stitch up the side seams. Turn the bag right side out and press.

5. Cut two 15" lengths of the pink, cream, and mauve silk ribbons. Make six folded roses as follows:

a. Fold down the right end of the ribbon.

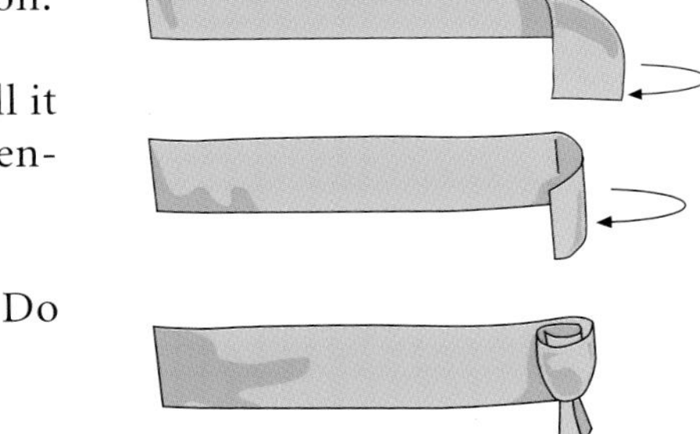

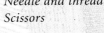

b. Fold the ribbon across once, then roll it four or five times to form a coiled center/stump.

c. Stitch the stump to secure the roll. Do not cut the thread.

d. Fold back all the ribbon on the left. Tilt the coiled ribbon stump (this puts "air" between the folded layers) and roll it across the diagonal fold of the turned back ribbon.

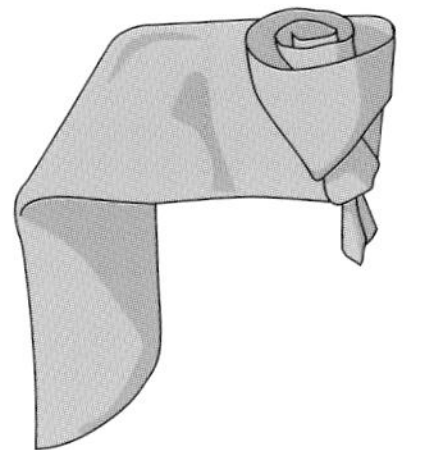

e. Stitch the stump to secure all the ribbon folds.

f. Repeat the folding and rolling until all but 2" of the ribbon is used. To finish, fold the end of the ribbon down and stitch the raw edge into the base of the stump.

6. Stitch one of each color rose together at their bases to make a rose cluster. Repeat.

7. Make three loops and streamer tails from 36" of green silk ribbon for each cluster. Stitch this below each cluster of roses. Stitch a pinback to each cluster.

8. Pin the clusters to the gift bag near the handles.

The following products were used for this project: Artemis Hand-Dyed Bias Cut Silk Ribbons, Wired Ribbon and Flower Braid from The Ribbon Club.

Materials:

13" x 26" piece heavy chintz fabric
34" cream striped wired ribbon, 1-1/2"-wide
32" cream flower trim
30" each - pink, cream, and mauve bias cut silk ribbon, 1-1/2"-wide
2 yards green bias cut silk, 1"-wide
2 pinbacks, 1"
Sewing machine
Needle and thread
Scissors

Ellie's Beginner Project

Ellie Joos

Ellie Joos is vice-president of the Offray Ribbon Co. She makes frequent appearances on craft and home television programs and teaches ribbon technique classes at trade and consumer shows. She has authored two ribbon books.

Ribbon Circus Animal Party Bag

The circus is coming to town in the form of this colorful bag that can be used to carry a gift and later become a handy bag for a child's room. This bag uses premade circus animals and can be easily assembled by a child with some adult supervision. Leo the Lion does a balancing act on a ribbon beach ball while Allie the Elephant tiptoes across a ribbon tightrope. Milo and Molly Monkey swing up above, while Gerry Giraffe watches the action from below.

Instructions:

1. Glue the ribbon circus animal heads to the safari animal bodies.

2. Cut the 7/8"-wide ribbon in half. Turn the short ends under and stitch. Stitch along the long edge with a gathering stitch and gather the ribbon, pulling it into a circle shape. Overlap the short ends and stitch together. Repeat with the other half. Glue a pompom to the center.

3. Cut the 3/8"-wide ribbon in half and glue diagonally across the bag, front and back.

4. Punch holes in the top of the bag and thread the three 1/8"-wide ribbons through the holes, tying a bow in front.

5. Glue the ball and circus animals to the bag, front and back.

The following products were used for this project: Offray Ribbon Circus Animals, Offray Double Face Satin Ribbon, Offray Grosgrain Ribbon, FibreCraft Safari Animals.

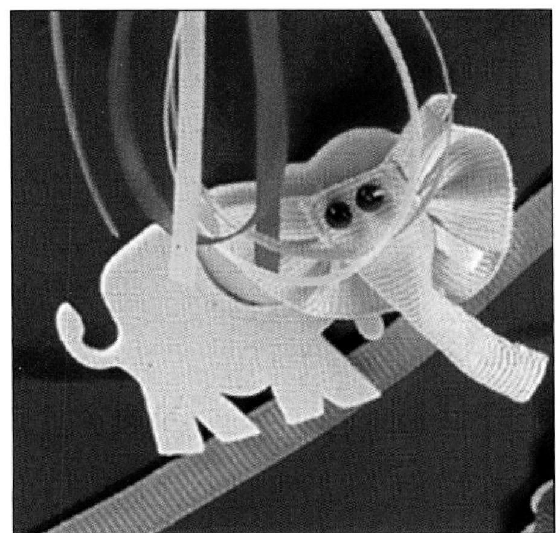

Materials:

7" x 10" gift bag
Ribbon circus animals of choice
1 yard each of 3 colors double face satin ribbon, 1/8"-wide
1/2 yard grosgrain ribbon, 3/8"-wide, for tight rope
2/3 yard grosgrain ribbon, 7/8"-wide, for lion's ball
1/2" pompom
Hole punch
Needle and thread
Glue

Ellie's Intermediate Project

Poinsettia Gift Box

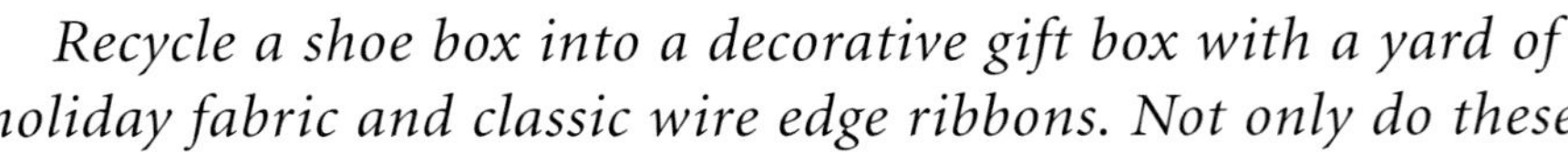

Recycle a shoe box into a decorative gift box with a yard of holiday fabric and classic wire edge ribbons. Not only do these ribbons make great dimensional bows, but with the techniques shown here, you can make a ribbon poinsettia to last from year to year.

Instructions:

Box

1. Spray paint the inside of the box and lid with gold paint.

2. Wrap the box and lid with fabric and glue to secure.

3. Using the gold edge sheer ribbon, crisscross across the top of the lid and glue to the inside edge. Repeat on the box.

4. Glue two rows of gold metallic ribbon around the inner edge of the box to hide the raw edges of the fabric and sheer ribbon.

Floral Arrangement

1. To make the five poinsettia petals:

a. Cut the 1-1/2"-wide ivory wire edge ombre ribbon into five 6"-8" lengths and fold in half.

b. Fold the corners at a right angle on each end. Stitch along the folded corners and across the short edge of the ribbon using a running or gathering stitch.

c. Gently pull the thread to gather the ribbon and knot the thread to secure the gathers.

d. Trim the excess ribbon from the folded corners and open to form the petal.

Petals

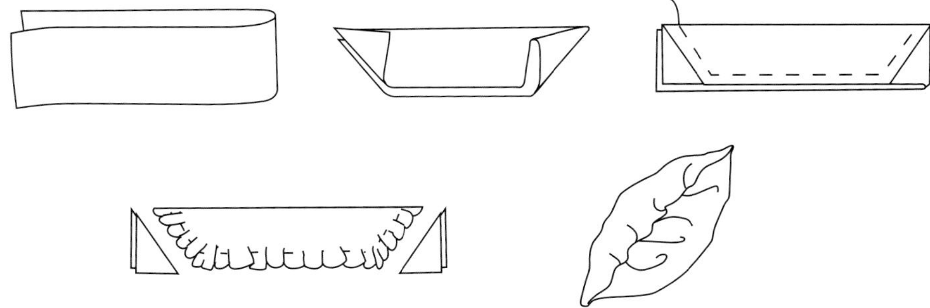

2. To make the stamens, cut the 3/8"-wide gold metallic wire edge ribbon into ten even lengths. Make a knot in the center of each and fold the ends down. Repeat and glue or wire all the stamens together.

3. Glue the poinsettia petals around the stamens.

continued on page 60

Materials:

Ribbon:

1-1/3 yard ivory wire edge ombre, 1-1/2"-wide
28" ivory wire edge ombre, 7/8"-wide
1-1/3 yard dark green wire edge taffeta, 1-1/2"-wide
1 yard gold metallic wire edge, 3/8"-wide
3 yards gold edge sheer, 1-1/2"-wide

76" gold grosgrain, 5/8"-wide
1 yard poinsettia fabric
Shoe box
Spray glue
Gold spray paint
Hot glue gun
Polyester fiberfill
Needle and thread
Floral wire

4. To make the five leaves:

a. Cut the green ribbon into five 9-1/2" lengths.

b. Make a knot in one end and pull snugly towards the end. At the opposite end, pull out the wire and gather the length down to the knot.

c. Fold the ribbon in half crosswise. Roll the ribbon down to meet the knot.

d. Wrap wire around the ribbon end and knot to secure. Shape the points.

Leaves

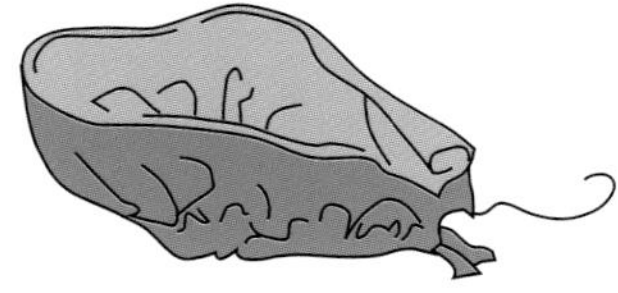

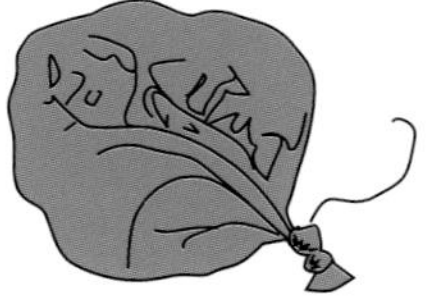

5. Glue the leaves to poinsettia, spacing evenly.

6. Make a bow from the sheer ribbon and glue the box to the box lid. Glue the poinsettia to the box lid.

7. To make the berries:

a. Cut the 7/8"-wide ivory ombre ribbon into 4" lengths.

b. Overlap the cut ends to form a ring and glue.

c. Sew gathering stitches along one edge of the ribbon and pull it tightly.

d. Knot the thread and turn inside out to hide the stitches.

e. Stuff with fiberfill. Gather the remaining edge, pull tightly, and knot the thread.

Berries

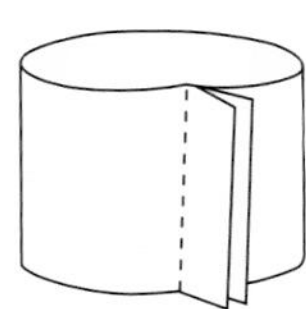

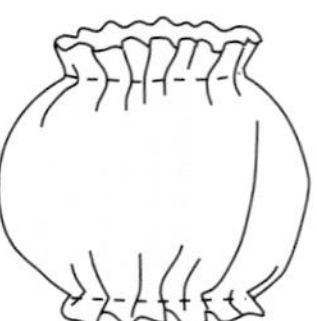

8. Glue the berries to the box lid.

9. Coil floral wire around a pencil and glue to the box lid, creating a vine.

The following products were used for this project: Offray Ribbons - Wire Edge Ombre, Wire Edge Taffeta, Wire Edge Gold Metallic Grosgrain, Divine Sheer, Gold Grosgrain.

Ribbon-Covered Wedding Heart Box

Ellie's Advanced Project

Every bride will treasure this lovely gift box. Apply lengths of ribbons to a simple box, add a nosegay of ribbon roses cascading over the side, and you have a memento box for the bride to save precious items from her special day.

Materials:

Paper maché heart box, 10" x 9" x 4"
White spray paint
Spray glue
Hot glue gun
Needle and thread
Ribbon for box:
- *1-1/2 yard white single face satin, 7/8"-wide*
- *1-1/2 yard antique white single face satin, 5/8"-wide*
- *1-1/3 yard woven Keepsake ribbon, 1-1/2"-wide*
- *42" woven Memento ribbon, 1-1/2"-wide*
- *39" lace edge satin, 7/8"-wide*
- *1 yard woven Flora ribbon, 5/8"-wide*

Ribbon for floral arrangement:
- *1-3/4 yard ivory wire edge ombre, 7/8"-wide*
- *1 yard ivory wire edge ombre, 1-1/2"-wide*
- *1-1/2 yard white wire edge sheer Arabesque, 7/8"-wide*
- *1 yard white wire edge sheer Arabesque, 1-1/2"-wide*
- *1 yard green double face satin, 1-1/2"-wide*

1 package each white and cream ribbon asters with pearl bead centers
1 package small white ribbon roses

Instructions:

Box

1. Spray paint the box and lid white, inside and out.

2. Cut 31" lengths of the white single face satin, Memento, lace edge satin, and Keepsake ribbons. Starting at the top of the box, glue the ribbons in the order given around the box with spray glue or glue of your choice, butting the edges.

3. Cut 31" of Flora and antique white single face satin ribbon and set aside.

4. For the box lid, cut the remaining ribbons into strips to fit and glue in this order from left to right, butting the edges: Keepsake, antique white satin, Flora, white satin, Memento, white satin, lace edge satin, antique white satin, Keepsake, antique white satin, Flora.

5. Glue the set aside lengths of Flora and antique white satin around the edge of the box lid, covering the cut ends of the ribbons on the box lid.

Floral Arrangement

1. Make three pulled wire gathered roses:

a. Cut two 18" lengths of 1-1/2"-wide ivory wire edge ombre ribbon (one for each rose). Cut one 12" length of 7/8"-wide ivory wire edge ombre ribbon.

b. Knot one end and pull the knot firmly toward the end to secure. On the other end, pull one wire, gathering the ribbon along that edge. Continue gathering until the full length is completely ruffled.

c. Wrap the gathered ribbon around the knotted end. Continue wrapping tightly so the ribbon flares out.

d. Tie the wires together and trim any excess ribbon.

Gathered Rose

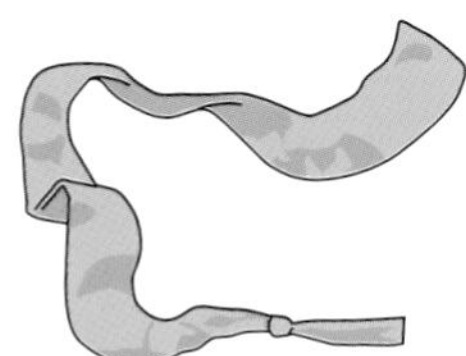
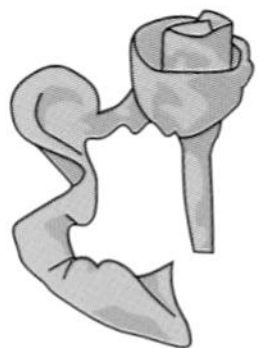
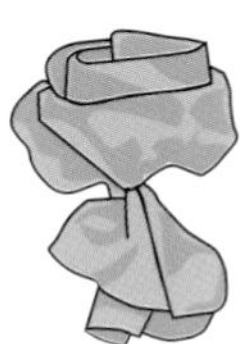

2. Make five folded roses:

a. From the 7/8"-wide ivory wire edge ombre ribbon, cut two 12" lengths and three 9" lengths.

b. Form the rose center by folding down one end of the ribbon and roll the folded end a few turns. Stitch the base to secure.

c. Form the petals by folding the top edge away from you, parallel to the center. Roll across the fold, loosely at the top and tighter at the base, forming a cone shape. Stitch the base to secure. Continue to fold, roll, stitch, and shape.

d. Wrap floral wire around the base to secure.

Folded Rose

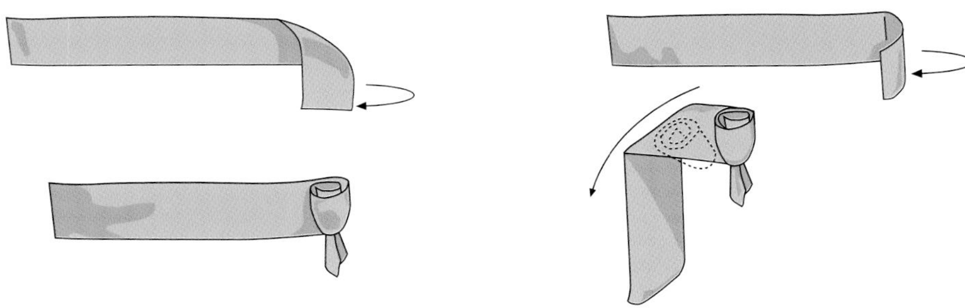

3. Make seven folded leaves:

a. Cut seven 4-1/2" lengths of green double face satin ribbon. Cut one 4-1/2" tail.

b. Mark the center of the ribbon and fold the ends diagonally to the center mark.

c. At the bottom edge, fold each side toward the center.

d. Pleat the lower edge to the center, twist, and secure with floral tape.

Folded Leaf

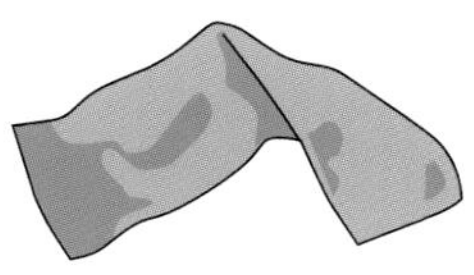
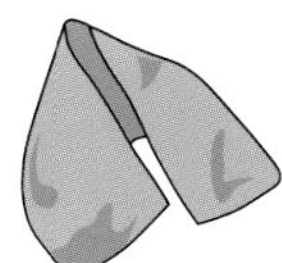
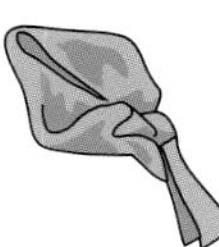

4. Cut three 12" lengths and three 9" lengths of 7/8"-wide sheer ribbon. Set aside two of the 9" lengths for tails. Pinch the center of each ribbon and form loops. Make three two-loop bows with tails from the 12" lengths and one one-loop bow with a tail from the 9" length. Use the set aside 9" lengths as tails, cut with a chevron on the ends.

5. Cut one 8" length, one 22" length, and one 6" length of 1-1/2"-wide sheer ribbon. Make a one-loop bow with a tail from the 8" length, one four-loop bow from the 22" length, and a 6" double tail.

6. Glue the floral arrangement to the box lid, starting in the upper left and cascading down the right to the side of the box. Glue the leaves first, then the bows, then the ribbon roses. Finish by gluing the packaged asters throughout the design and over the edge of the lid onto the box side.

The following Offray ribbons were used for this project: Single Face Satin, Keepsake, Memento, Lace Edge Satin, Flora, Wire Edge Ombre, Arabesque, Double Face Satin, Premade Ribbon Asters, Premade Ribbon Roses.

Pear Boxes

Judi's Beginner Project

Judi Kauffman

Judi is a versatile and prolific craft and needlework designer whose favorite techniques include needlepoint, quilting, bead embellishment, rubber stamping, crochet, and all kinds of embroidery. Born into a family of artists who made everything from scratch, she has been stitching, knitting, and sewing since she was small. Judi considers it her life's mission to convince people that they are creative, a goal that has led her to write and design for a wide variety of craft and needlework magazines, to write and produce videos, and develop kits for manufacturers. She is the author of the book, Memory Crafting.

Create an elegant textured gift box that can be used after the holidays to store treasures, jewelry, or sewing supplies. The boxes shown feature a pear on top, but you can choose a different fruit, ornament, or small toy instead. The pear appears to be "perched" on the lid, but it is firmly attached with wire from the bottom. The texture is created using rubber bands! The technique is easy enough for beginners and children.

Instructions:

Read all manufacturer's instructions for each product before you begin.

1. Protect the work surface and wear latex gloves while working with the inks - they dry fast and are permanent.

2. Using cosmetic sponge wedges, apply red ink to the lid and base of the box and all surfaces of the fruit, including the leaves. Add a second coat for opaque color. You can also apply ink to the inside of the box and the lid if you'd like.

3. With a second cosmetic sponge wedge, brush black ink over the surfaces to "antique" the pieces. Dab the excess on plastic or paper and apply very little ink - the sponge should be almost dry.

4. Put the rubber bands around the tennis ball, overlapping them crisscross fashion. Heat the foam circle and press the rubber band covered ball against it to emboss a (reverse) pattern/texture on the foam. *Note: The foam can be reheated to create a different texture or kept as is to use for other projects.*

The moldable foam block embossed with the texture of the rubber band covered tennis ball.

5. Lay a clean piece of paper on the work table. With the metallic gold ink, randomly stamp the reverse foam circle pattern on the pieces. Stamp gently so the red and black show through. While the ink is wet, sprinkle clear embossing powder over the surface. Fold the paper at one side to pour the excess embossing powder back in the jar. Emboss the texture with a heat tool. Let the pieces dry for a few minutes.

6. Pat the ink pad against the rubber band covered ball (green for the large box, black for the small box). Use the inked ball to randomly stamp crisscrossed lines on the pieces. Emboss as in step 5, using iridescent embossing powder for the large box and clear embossing powder for the small box. Pour the excess powder back in the jar.

7. When all the pieces are dry, pierce a small hole in the center of the box lid. Poke the wire at the base of the fruit through the hole, turn the wire across and bend it into a spiral. Glue the felt or synthetic suede piece inside the lid to cover the wire (this will hold the fruit in place).

The following products were used for this project: Ranger DecorIt Inks, Tsukineko Encore Ink Pads, Tsukineko Ultimate Metallic Ink Pad, Top Boss Embossing Powder, Magic Stamp (PenScore) Moldable Foam Block from Clearsnap, Personal Stamp Exchange Embossing Heat Tool, Beacon Kids Choice Glue.

Materials:

Paper maché boxes: round 4", round 7", or as desired
Permanent inks: Primary Red, Black
Ink pads: Green (large box), Black (small box), Metallic Gold (both boxes)
Embossing powder: Clear, Iridescent
Cosmetic sponge wedges
2" round piece of moldable foam block
Latex gloves (very important)
Old tennis ball or other ball
20-30 rubber bands
Fruit with stiff wire at base (or other dimensional embellishment made of plastic, foam, or wood with a pick at the bottom)
2" circles of red felt or synthetic suede (1 per box)
Embossing heat tool
1 yard wired gold cord or narrow wire edge ribbon
Glue

Judi's Intermediate Project

Fabric Box

From an itty bitty box for a pair of earrings to a jumbo one filled with a big bag of caramel popcorn, it's hard to stop making fabric boxes once you get started. They can be soft and droopy (padded with fusible fleece batting) or stand tall (stiffened by fusible stabilizer). They can be plain or fancy. Use any fabric you have on hand or buy something special. The box shown features photo transfers of vintage postcards. The embellishments can be sewn or glued in place. Sew buttons or charms in place if they are valuable or if you might want to remove them in the future.

Instructions:

1. To determine the size and shape of your fabric box, refer to Diagram A.

2. Add 1/2" seam allowances on all sides of both patterns and cut two paper patterns. Cut one in half. Use pattern #1 to cut fabric for the outside of the box. Use pattern #2 to cut two halves of the lining.

Diagram A - Box

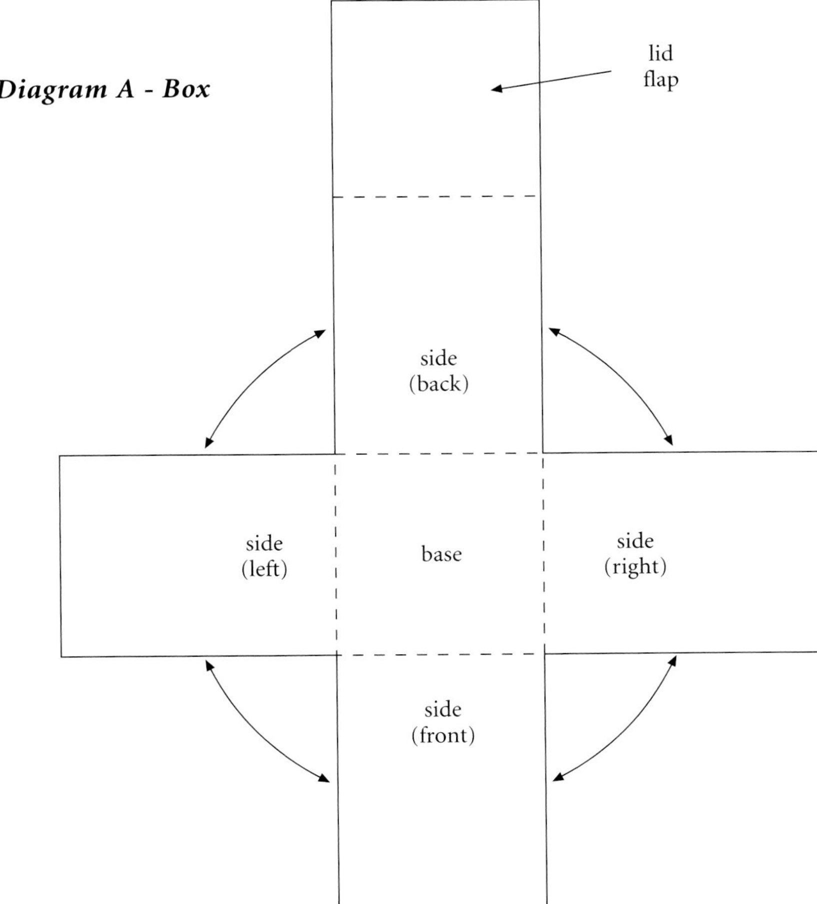

Materials:

Fabric for box and lining (see Diagram A to determine amount)

Note: For boxes made with photo transfers, the fabric must be light colored.

Sewing thread

Bead needle

Fabric photo transfer paper

Old postcards, photographs, or other copyright-free images for transfers

Dimensional embellishments - charms, buttons, silk flowers, ribbon, lace

Optional: Fusible fleece to pad the sides and/or fusible stabilizer to stiffen them

Paper

Pencil

Straight edge

Fabric glue

Illustration board (see Diagram B to determine the amount)

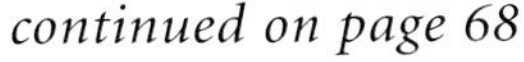

continued on page 68

Diagram B - Lining

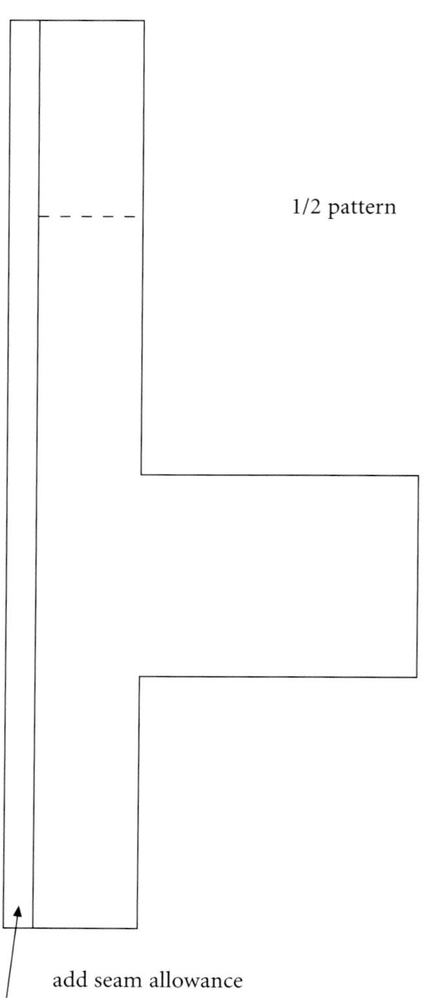

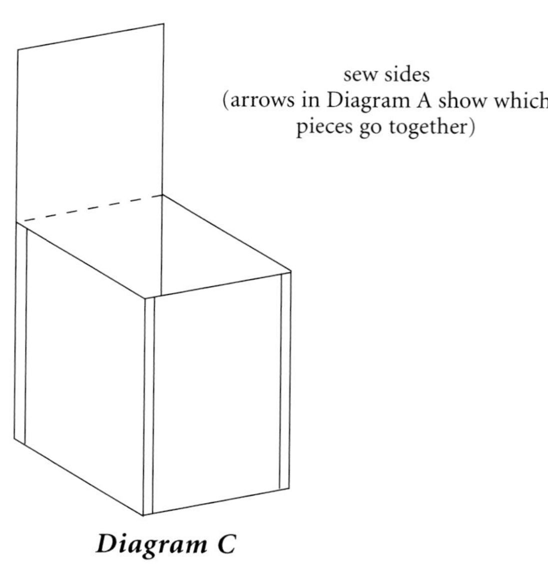

Diagram C

3. With right sides together, sew the lining pieces together, leaving an opening 1/3 the length of the lining seam for turning.

4. If making a stiff box, fuse stabilizer to the back of the box fabric *before* the photo transfers are ironed on.

5. Iron the photo transfers onto one or more sides of the box fabric and on the lid if desired. Create a collage using family photos or make transfers from vintage postcards or other copyright-free illustrations. For a padded box, follow the manufacturer's directions to lightly fuse fleece to the wrong side of the box fabric *after* the photo transfers are ironed on. Keep the iron away from the photo transfers.

I added pretty gold embellishments around the images on the lid.

6. Sew the lace, beads, charms, and other embellishments in place.

7. With right sides together, sew the four side seams on the box. Leave the box wrong side out.

8. Repeat with the lining. Turn the lining right side out and put it inside the box (the right sides will be together). Baste or pin around the lid flap and top edges of the box. Sew the pieces together.

9. Clip the corners. Be careful not to cut through the fabric when clipping the corner at the lid flap.

10. Turn the box right side out through the opening in the lining.

11. Using a press cloth to protect the photo transfers, carefully iron the edges to straighten the sides. Sew or glue the opening in the lining closed.

Options:

- Make a closure with ribbon or decorative braid or a button, snap, or tassel.
- Change the base and make a box shaped like a hexagon or pentagon.
- Omit the lid flap, add a handle, and make a basket.

The following products were used for this project: Photo Effects Fabric Photo Transfer Paper from Hues, Inc., Creative Corners 24K Corners from Creative Beginnings, Mill Hill Seed and Bugle beads, Crafter's Choice Fusible Stabilizer and Fusible Fleece from HTC, Beacon Fabri-Tac Glue.

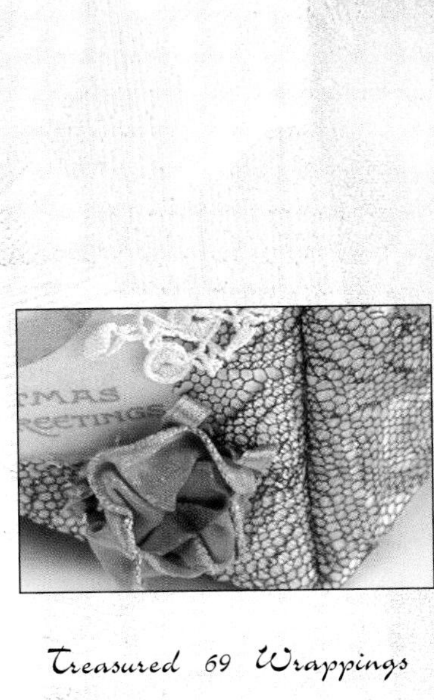

Judi's Advanced Project

Furoshiki (Wrapping Cloth)

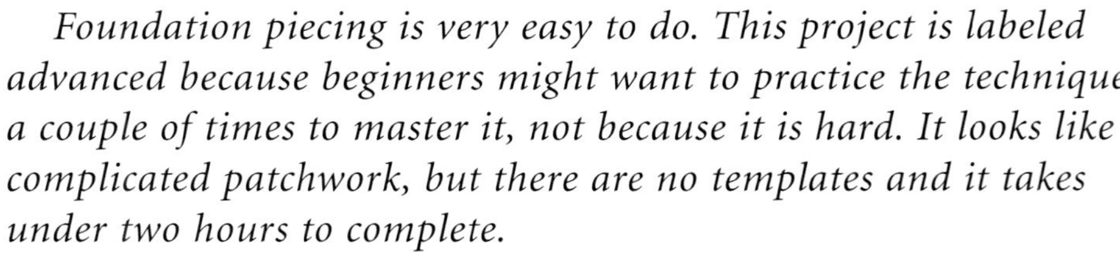

Foundation piecing is very easy to do. This project is labeled advanced because beginners might want to practice the technique a couple of times to master it, not because it is hard. It looks like complicated patchwork, but there are no templates and it takes under two hours to complete.

The furoshiki is a tote bag, shopping bag, and a gift wrap all in one. Traditionally furoshiki are used for everything from carrying lunch to presenting important gifts. I like to give a beautiful cloth tied around an assortment of fabrics to a friend who sews or quilts. An unlined furoshiki can become the center medallion of a quilt or bedspread or the front of a pillow after it is used as a wrap.

Once you know how big the item is that you wish to wrap, you can determine the size furoshiki to make. Soft fabrics tie best. The larger the finished size, the easier it is to use heavier fabrics. For tiny projects, use silk or lightweight cotton and synthetics and pin the fabrics in place to hold them as you sew.

If you want to enjoy the furoshiki when you're not using it to wrap and carry something, spread it out on a table as a centerpiece, drape it over a chair, or if it's 54" or larger, wear it folded into a triangle as a shawl.

Materials:

Fabric scraps or purchased yardage (amount determined by size desired)
Sewing thread in compatible color (neutral dark gray works well)
Lining fabric square (size determined by Diagram A)
Translucent quilt block piecing material (size determined by Diagram A)
Pencil
Straight edge
Muslin or old sheet to determine amount of fabric needed (see Diagram A)
Charms, beads, other embellishments (optional)

Instructions:

Read and follow the foundation piecing directions on the piecing material package.

Think of the fabric pieces as butterfly wings. Each piece that gets added after the first one is like closed wings (face to face). After sewing on the straight line, the wings are opened out (mirror image) side by side. A piece that will end up at an uphill angle to the left will start out at an uphill angle to the right.

1. To determine the size of the furoshiki, place the item to be wrapped in the center of a piece of muslin or old sheet and follow the instructions in Diagram A. Cut a test square from muslin, fold in the corners, and tie (see step 8). Adjust the size of the cloth if needed before cutting from "real" fabric.

2. Enlarge the pattern block (Diagram B). Hand or machine baste two or more pieces of foundation piecing together for a large furoshiki. Trace all the lines and numbers onto the foundation piecing material using a pencil and straight edge.

3. Set your sewing machine to 18 stitches per inch. Following the foundation piecing manufacturer's directions, add the fabric pieces in numerical order to complete the square. Cut along the dotted line.

4. Use the finished square as a pattern to cut the backing fabric.

5. Carefully remove the basting threads and tear away the foundation piecing material along the lines perforated by the sewing.

6. With right sides together, sew the backing and pieced square together. Leave an opening on one side.

7. Trim the seam allowances and clip the corners. Turn right side out. Close the opening with small stitches, fabric glue, or fusible tape.

8. Sew optional embellishments (beads or charms) to the corners marked with an X on Diagram B. Use sewing thread doubled in the needle for strength. Bury knots and thread between the beads in the seam allowances so they don't show.

9. Center the gift to be wrapped on the lining side of the furoshiki. Fold in the plain corners first, then fold in and tie the decorated corners.

The following products were used for this project: Fun-dation Translucent Quilt Block Piecing Material from HTC, Sulyn Industries Beads.

Diagram A

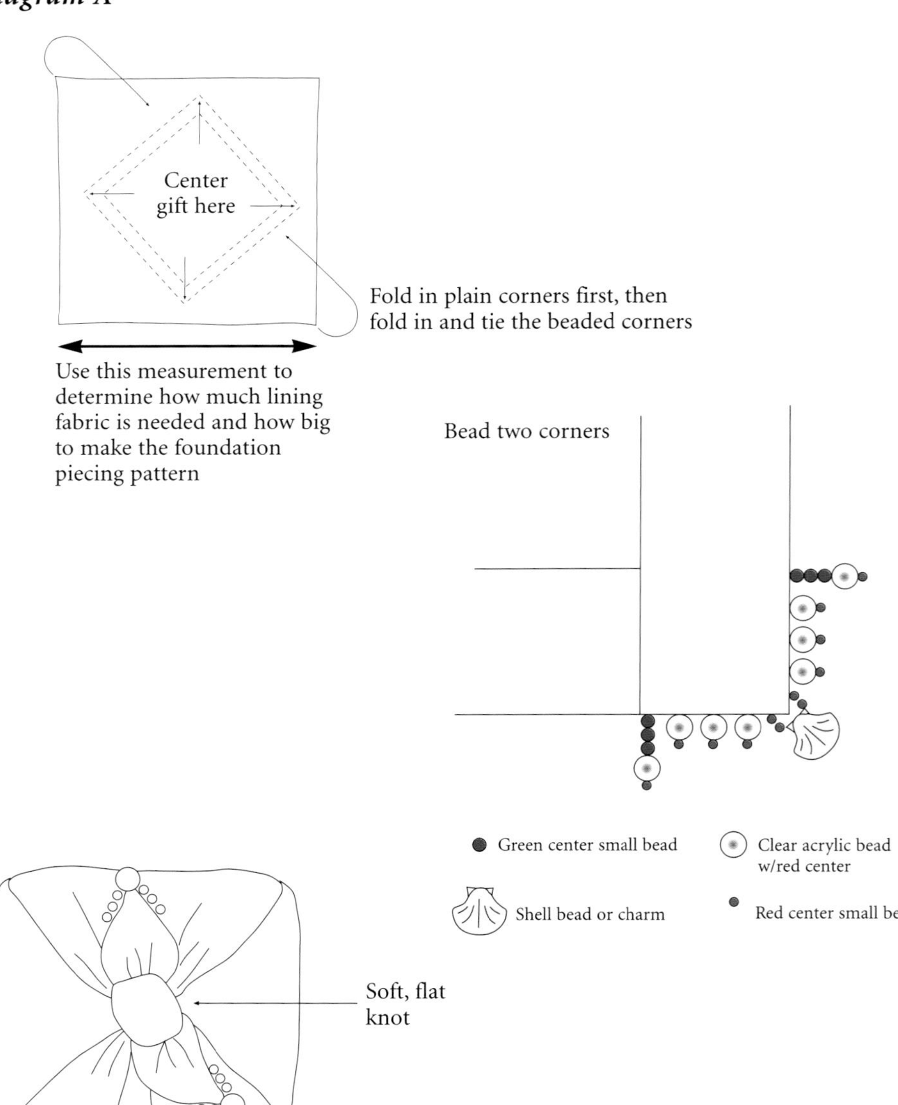

Diagram B Enlarge or reduce to size required

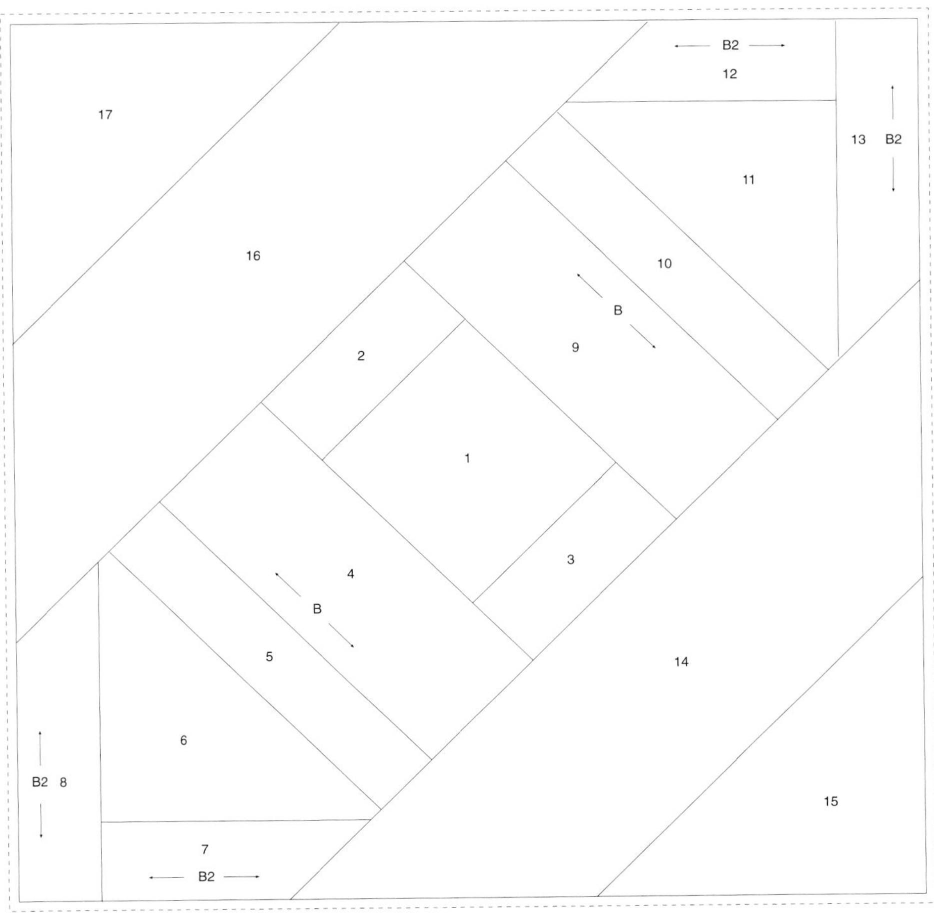

Foundation Piecing Pattern
As shown (a symmetrical design)

Pieces #4 + #9, #7, #8, #12, #13 = Fabric B
Pieces #15 + #17, #6 + #11 = Fabric A
Piece #1 = Fabric C
Pieces #2 + #3 = Fabric D
Pieces #5 + #10 = Fabric E
Pieces #14 + #16 = Fabric F
B = Section #1 of border print
B2 = Section #2 of border print

* *Arrows indicate the direction of the strip from the border print*

Linda's Beginner Project

Linda McGehee

Linda is the author of several award-winning books including Texture with Textiles. *Her most recent book is* Creating Texture with Textiles. *She has designed garments for the prestigious Fairfield Fashion Show, Statements, Capitol Imports, and* Better Homes & Gardens.

Memory Tote

Use a lightweight woven rug with fringe to create a memory tote for mom or grandmother. I made the decorative "photo pockets" with computer printer fabric, but you can use photo transfer paper too. This is the perfect all-purpose tote for vacations, shopping sprees, or sewing and quilting conventions. It is a quick project you can make in an evening. So simple to make and so much fun to carry!

Instructions:

1. Fold each fringed end right sides together 1". Stitch near the fringe and near the top edge to hold in place. The two fringed rug ends become the top (opening) of the tote.

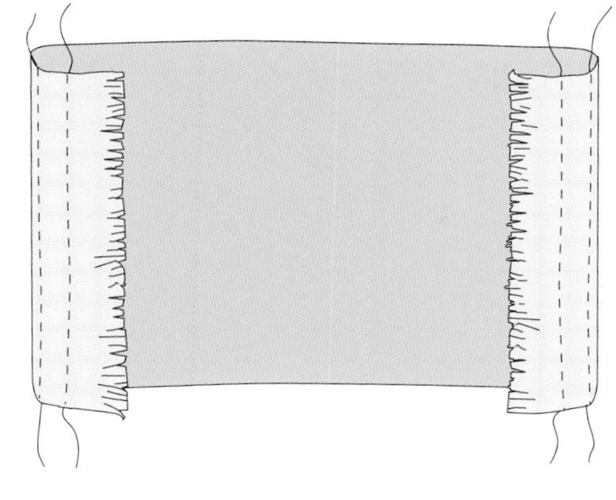

2. Fold the rug in half, matching the folded fringed ends. Now that you know the size and shape of the tote, it is easy to determine the pocket placement. Mark the position for the pockets with pins or a marking pencil. Place the pockets above the midsection rather than towards the bottom. Once the tote is full, the bottom becomes wider than you think. It is better for the pockets to be positioned toward the top so the contents won't fall out.

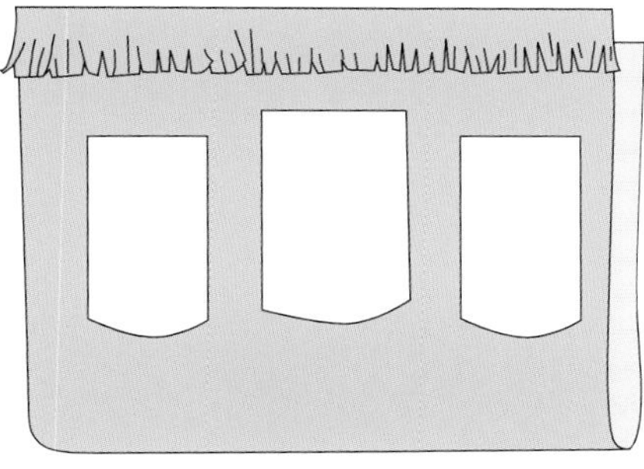

3. Open the rug before stitching the pockets. To make the memory pockets using computer images, scan existing photos with a computer scanner or have your 35mm film developed on CD Rom and import to a document or use a digital camera and import to a document. When you are satisfied with the image, print it on computer printer fabric, following the directions on the package. Or transfer photos to fabric with photo transfer paper. To be certain the photo is permanent, spray with a fabric sealant. The clear matte finish protects the fabric design. *Note: Some computer printer fabric may not be permanent. Be certain the computer fabric you purchase is permanent and the design will not fade in the rain or washing.*

4. To stabilize the pockets, interface with fusible interfacing. Position the photo right side down on the ironing board and place the pebble side of the interfacing down on the wrong side of the computer fabric. Fuse the layers with the wool setting on a steam iron.

5. Fold under the top edge of each pocket and stitch to secure. Fold under and press the sides and bottom of each pocket. Position them on the side of the tote. Stitch in place to secure. For more design, stitch rickrack or other trim around each pocket. Another option is decorative stitches from your sewing machine.

continued on page 76

Materials:

Lightweight woven rug with fringe, approximately 20" x 36"
1-3/4 yard belting or webbing
Thread to match
Computer with printer
Computer printer fabric
Note: You can also use photo transfer.
Fusible interfacing
Rickrack or other trim
Fabric sealant

6. Divide and cut the belting in half to form two straps. Make any length adjustments now. Open the rug right side down. Place the straps on the wrong side (the inside of the tote) with the cut ends facing the upper edge of the tote. The ends of one strap will curve around to the top. Stitch from the right side (outside) of the tote, following previous stitch lines.

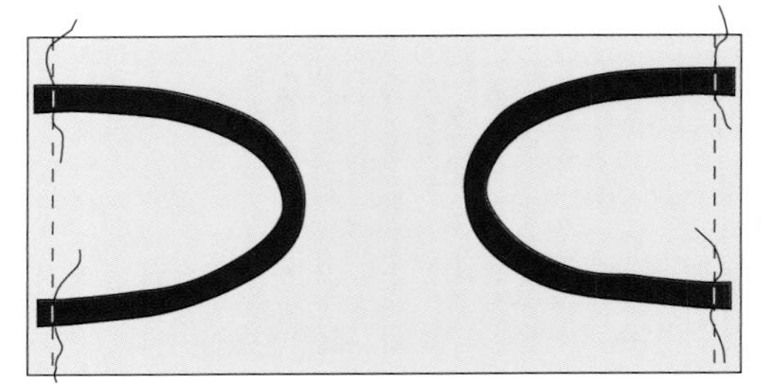

7. Pull the straps out of the tote. The straps should cover the cut ends. Stitching from the right side (outside), secure the straps a second time.

8. Fold the tote in half as before and stitch the sides closed. Because of the bulk it may be difficult to stitch all the way to the top. It is perfectly fine to stop the stitching at the fringe.

The following products were used for this project: June Tailor Computer Printer Fabric, Krylon Fabric Sealant.

Jewelry Pouch

Linda's Intermediate Project

The jewelry pouch is a simple project that takes very little time to do. The embellishment requires the most time, so keep it simple and make several of these for gifts at Mother's Day, birthdays, Christmas, showers, or other special occasions. Use leftovers from your thread and fabric collection or start from scratch.

Materials:

2 pieces fabric 10" x 10" for outside of pouch and lining (Use the same fabric for both or contrast the colors for variety)
Polyester fleece, 10" x 10"
Thread to match
12" purchased corded piping
Heavier threads for decoration
Basting or bobbin thread
Variegated decorative thread for the sewing machine needle
4" metal eyeglass case frame

Instructions:

1. Sandwich the fleece between the wrong sides of the outside fabric and the lining. The texture of the fleece causes the layers to stick to it.

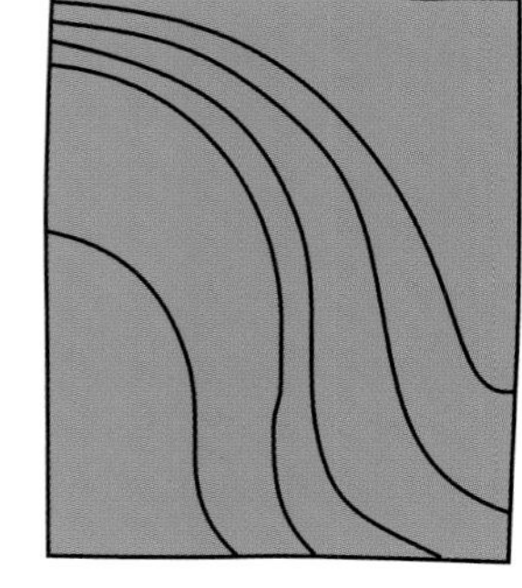

2. When the project is finished, the 1" area along the top won't show and the fabric will be divided in half (about the size of an eyeglass case). Consider this when planning the embellishment. Use a marking pen or chalk marker to draw the design on the outside fabric. I usually try to make my embellishment asymmetrical. The finished look is more appealing and I don't have to plan so accurately! Begin at one corner and draw diagonal wavy lines.

3. Fill a bobbin with basting or bobbin thread. Thread the machine with variegated decorative thread using a topstitching needle. Use the braiding foot to add the embellishments. A hole at the front of the foot is large enough to guide a small braid, heavier twisted threads, ribbon, yarn, or cord, making this couching technique a simple embellishment. Slide the heavier threads through the hole in the foot.

My stitch preference is the multi-step zigzag or darning stitch. Alter the stitch width to the same width as the twisted threads, approximately 1.5 to

Change the length to 1.5. As you begin stitching, the foot guides the embellishing thread toward the needle, making couching a very simple task. It is very easy to sew rows and rows of heavier decorative threads with very little effort. The foot does the guiding while you turn the fabric.

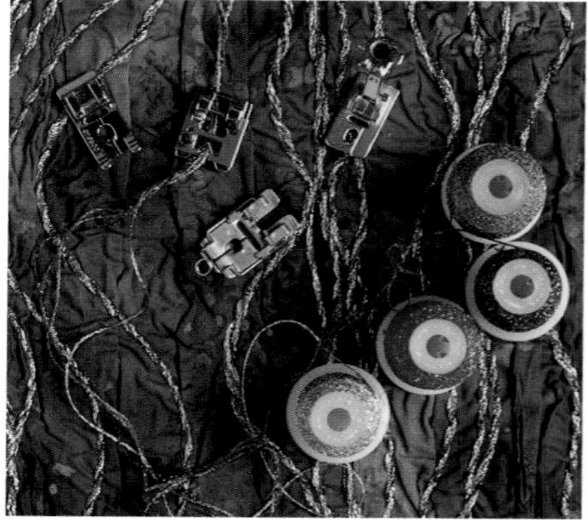

4. Meander over the fabric, fleece, and lining sandwich, creating the desired look. Sometimes a few rows of decoration is simple enough, other times it may be more fun to add lots of rows. Use contrasting colors to make the design bold or blend the colors of thread with the fabric for a more subtle appearance.

5. Once the design is complete, attach the corded piping to the lining side at the upper edge, keeping the cut edges together. Logically, this seems backwards. In the finished jewelry pouch, the corded piping will be flipped to the front. Stitch the corded piping in position with the piping foot and the needle moved slightly to the right.

6. To form the casing for the metal frame, fold the right sides of the outside fabric together 1" from the cut edge. Tuck under the seam allowance and stitch in the ditch along the corded piping to hold the seam allowance under. Another alternative is edgestitching.

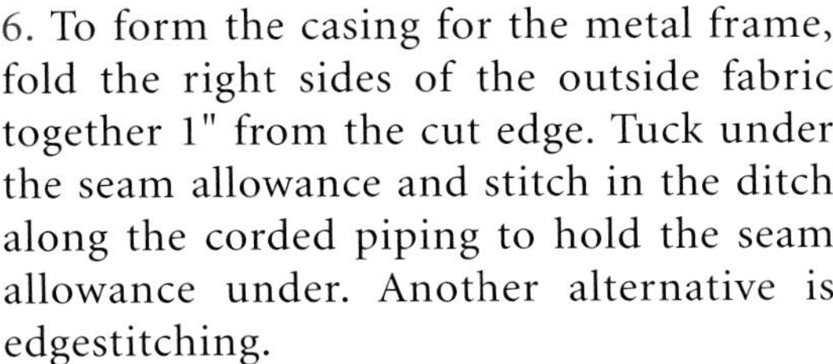

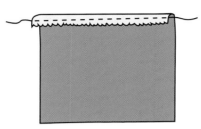

7. Fold the pouch in half lengthwise, with right sides together. Insert the frame from each open end with the curves facing each other. Push the frames in as snug as possible and pin to hold them tightly in place. Stitch down the side seam and across the bottom. Be certain the beginning stitches by the frame are secured. This is the area of the finished pouch that will have the most stress.

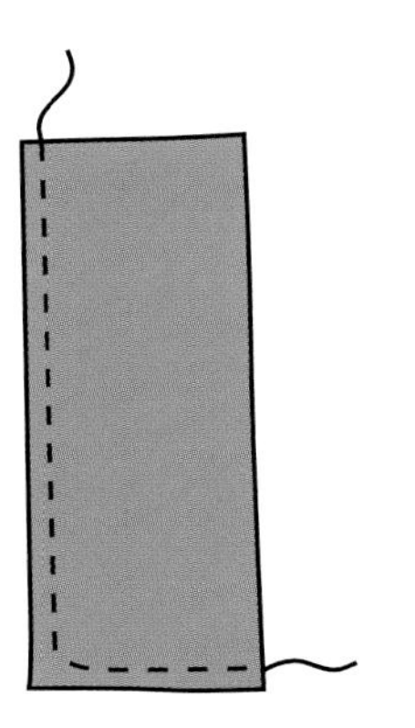

8. Turn the embellished side out to complete the jewelry pouch. Personalize with embroidery by hand or machine.

The following products were used for this project: Candlelight Decorative Tthread from YLI Corp., 4" Metal Eyeglass Frame by Ghee's.

Linda's Advanced Project

Cosmetic Case

Use a place mat to create a decorative cosmetic case for travel or everyday. It can double as a purse or satchel for other things girls need to stay organized. This is classified as an advanced project only because of the machine embroidery. If you use purchased appliqués, it's as simple as can be.

Instructions:

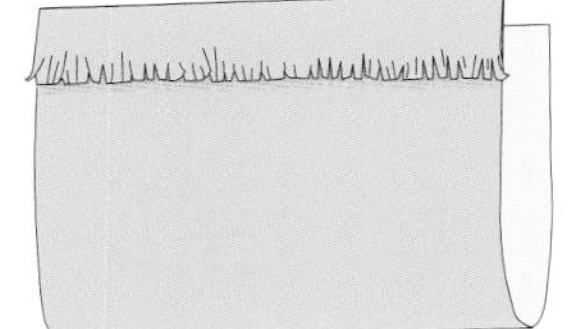

1. Fold each fringed end right sides together 1" and pin to secure. This will form the casing for the frame. Fold the place mat in half.

2. Now that you know the size and shape of the cosmetic case, it is easy to determine the design placement. Mark the position for the design with pins or a marking pencil. Place the design above the midpoint rather than towards the bottom. Once the case is full, the bottom becomes wider than you think. The design can be centered in the middle or towards the side.

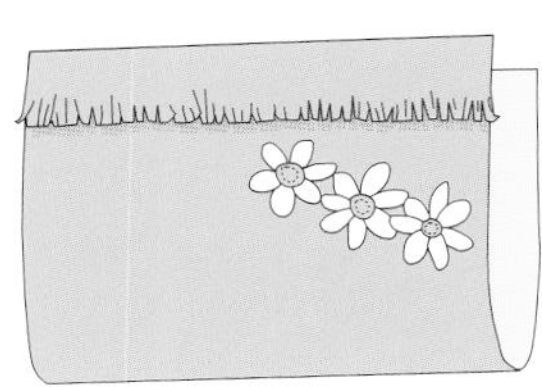

3. Open the place mat before stitching the embellishment. There are many purchased appliqués available that you can stitch directly to the place mat or you can use an embroidery disk.

4. Layer embellishments in a realistic design. Using the same color thread as the embroidery and the open toe foot, stitch the layers together while applying them to the place mat. The open toe foot allows you to see where you are stitching without hiding any curves and corners.

5. Once the embellishment design is complete, stitch the casing along each fringe end. Fold the place mat in half as before and stitch a pleat at the side bottom and continue up the side towards the casing. Stop stitching at the casing by the fringe and secure with a back tack stitch.

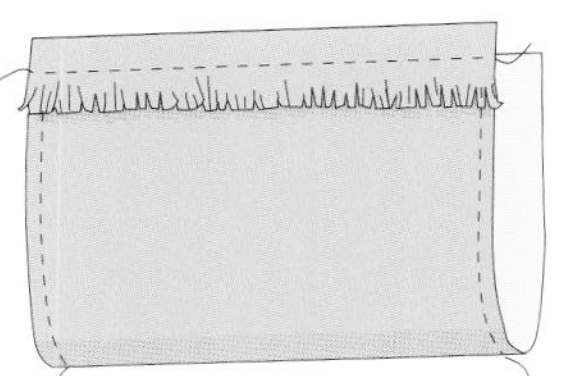

6. To hold the cosmetic case closed use a straight hex-open frame. The frame will hold the case open for easy visibility and closed to prevent things from falling out. The gathers will form when the frame goes through the place mat. On a shorter frame there are more gathers, on a longer frame there are fewer. The frames fit together much like a door hinge. Slide the frame through the casing, matching the opposite ends of the frame. Press these ends together to align the holes. Slide self-piloting rivets through the holes to secure the frame.

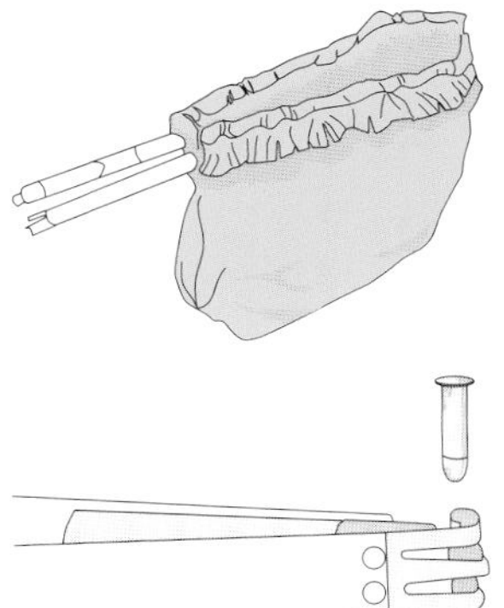

The following products were used for this project: Straight Hex-Open Frame from Ghee's, Cactus Punch Embroidery Digitizing Floral Dimensions Embroidery Disk (available from Ghee's or Cactus Punch).

Materials:

Place mat with fringe on each end
Thread to match
11" or 12" straight hex-open frame
Appliqué or embroidery design
Decorative thread for design

Vicki's Beginner Project

Vicki Schreiner

Vicki's innovative woodburning designs have created renewed interest in this ancient art. She has been painting and woodburning for 15 years and loves to find new ways to apply the technique to modern projects.

Tiny Treasures Teapot

This charming gift box would be perfect for a special necklace, earrings, watch, or a small collectible figure.

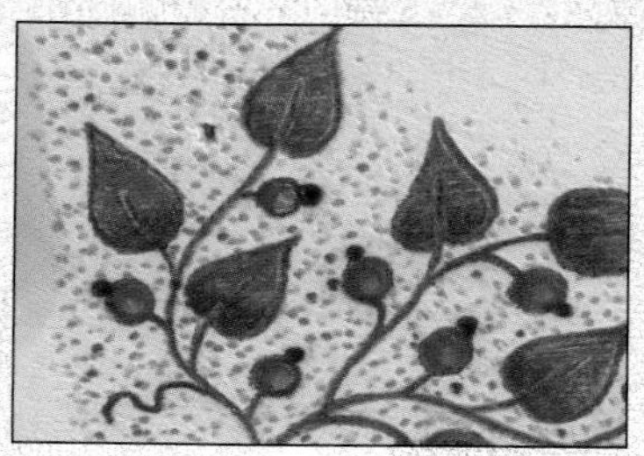

Instructions:

Patterns on page 84

1. Going with the grain of the wood, sand the entire surface with fine grit sandpaper.

2. Mix equal parts glaze base and Parchment acrylic paint. Work on one side at a time and brush the mixture on the entire box and lid. Wipe it off immediately with a soft cloth and let dry.

3. Lay the pattern on the front lower left area of the teapot and secure with small pieces of tape. Slide the transfer paper under the pattern, graphite side down. Go over the design lines with a ballpoint pen. Use a flexible ruler to transfer the lid design in the same manner.

4. Carefully follow the manufacturer's safety instructions when using the woodburning tool. Before plugging in the woodburner, remove the universal point and replace it with the cone point. Tighten with needlenose pliers. Plug in and let the burner heat up.

5. Practice a few woodburning strokes on the bottom of the teapot or on scrap wood before doing your project. Use slow, small sketching strokes instead of long continuous strokes. Don't use heavy pressure. The length of time you keep the tip of the woodburner on the wood determines the darkness, not the pressure. Let the heat do the work. To maintain even heat flow, keep the tip clean by occasionally dragging it across fine grit sandpaper.

6. Woodburn the outline of the design on the teapot and lid. Burn a dark dot at the top of each berry. Stipple a soft background for the berries and leaves by using a quick tapping motion to burn several dots very close together throughout the entire design. Stipple around the inside of the stripe on the lid in the same manner. Unplug the woodburner.

7. Darkly color all the leaves with Olive Green pencil. Shade the base of each leaf with Burnt Umber pencil directly on top of the green. Darkly color all the berries with the Crimson pencil and highlight them by adding a white pencil dot in the center of each. Darkly color the stripe on the lid with Crimson.

8. Apply two light coats of spray varnish to the entire teapot and lid to set the colors, letting dry between coats.

The following products were used for this project: Walnut Hollow Creative Woodburner #5567, Walnut Hollow Cone Point #5596, Walnut Hollow Teapot #11410, Walnut Hollow Oil Color Pencils, Walnut Hollow Graphite Transfer Paper, Delta Ceramcoat Glaze Base, Delta Ceramcoat Matte Interior Spray Varnish, Delta Ceramcoat Acrylic Paint.

Materials:

Woodburner & cone point
Wooden teapot, 6-3/8" x 5" x 4-1/8"
Oil color pencils: Olive Green, White, Burnt Umber, Alizarin Crimson
Graphite transfer paper
Glaze base
Matte interior spray varnish
Acrylic paint: Old Parchment
1/2" flat paintbrush
Soft cotton cloth
Fine grit sandpaper
Flexible ruler
Ballpoint pen
Needlenose pliers
Tape

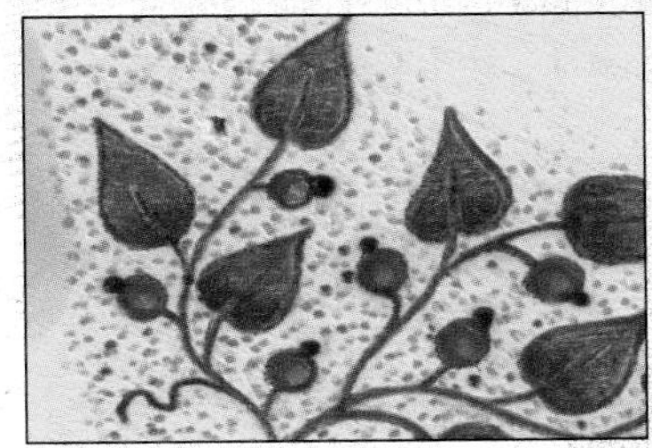

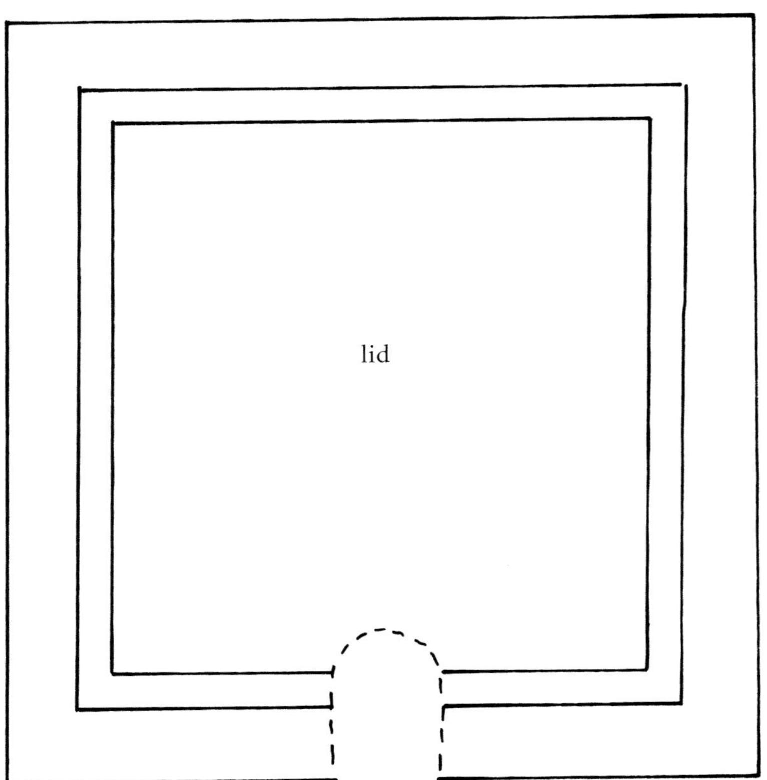
lid

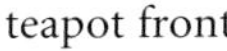
teapot front

Special Moments

Vicki's Intermediate Project

This would make an especially meaningful gift container for an anniversary gift, a gift for grandparents, or for a special sister.

Materials:

Woodburner & cone point
Wooden double recipe box, 7-5/8" x 3-5/8" x 5-7/8"
Oil color pencils: Olive Green, Blush Pink, Dark Brown
Glaze base
Matte interior spray varnish
Decoupage medium
Acrylic paints: Old Parchment, Village Green, Wedgwood Green
Stencil
Paper edgers
3/4" flat paintbrush
Soft cotton cloth
#2 pencil with eraser
Color copy of photograph to fit on box lid, approx. 4" x 6"
Fine grit sandpaper
Plain white paper
Scissors
Ruler
Needlenose pliers
Scrap pine or basswood for practice

Instructions:

1. Going with the grain of the wood, sand the entire surface with fine grit sandpaper.

2. Trace the scalloped edge pattern along the lid of the box about 1/8" from the bottom. Trace this edge all the way around the lid with a #2 pencil.

3. Mix equal parts glaze base and Parchment acrylic paint. Brush this mixture on one side of the box at a time. Apply to the entire lid above the scalloped edge. Wipe off immediately with a cotton cloth and let dry.

4. Mix equal parts glaze base with Village Green acrylic paint. Brush this mixture on one side of the box at a time. Apply to the lid and box below the scalloped edge. Wipe off immediately with a cotton cloth. Remove the divider from the inside of the box. Apply the mixture to the divider and wipe off immediately. Apply to the inside of the lip edge and the lid of the box, wiping off immediately. Let dry.

5. Mix equal parts glaze base and Wedgwood Green acrylic paint. Apply to the entire inside of the box and let dry. Replace the divider.

6. Draw an oval design (approx. 5-1/4" x 3-1/8") on a piece of plain paper and cut it out. Lay this oval pattern on back of the color photocopy. An easy way to check the oval placement is to hold the picture up to a light. On the back of the color photocopy, lightly trace around the oval with a #2 pencil and cut around the oval with the paper edgers. Set aside.

7. Lay the oval pattern centered on top of the lid. Lightly trace around it with a #2 pencil. Using the flower border pattern, trace eight individual flowers with leaves about 1/8" out from the traced oval. An easy way to do this is to trace the very left and very right flowers each with four leaves first, the very top and bottom flowers each with four leaves next, then place a flower with only two leaves between each of these. Erase the original oval pencil line.

8. Using the flower pattern and a #2 pencil, trace the flower design all around the lower portion of the box approximately 1/4" from the bottom edge.

9. Carefully follow the manufacturer's safety instructions when using the woodburning tool. Before plugging in the woodburner, remove the universal point and replace it with the cone point. Tighten with needlenose pliers. Plug in the woodburner and let it heat.

10. Practice a few strokes on a piece of scrap wood before doing your projects. Use slow, small sketching strokes instead of long continuous strokes. Don't use heavy pressure. The length of time you keep the tip of the woodburner on the wood determines the darkness, not the pressure. Let the heat do the work. To maintain even heat flow, keep the tip clean by occasionally dragging it across fine grit sandpaper.

11. Woodburn the outline of all the traced images on the box and lid. Hold the woodburner upright at the center of each flower to burn the center dot, then burn six dots around it. Apply tiny stippled dots on the lid directly below the scalloped edge by using a quick tapping motion to burn several dots very close together. Also burn stippled dots around the inside of the oval flower pattern approximately 1/2" in toward the center. Unplug the woodburner.

12. Darkly color all the flower petals with the Blush Pink pencil. Shade out from the center of each petal with the Dark Brown pencil directly on top of the pink. Darkly color all the leaves with Olive Green pencil.

13. Apply decoupage medium to the back of the cut out color photocopy and position it on the lid and press it in place. Let dry. Apply two coats of decoupage medium over the photocopy and stippling dots, letting it dry between coats.

14. Apply a coat of spray varnish over the entire box and let dry.

The following products were used for this project: Walnut Hollow Creative Woodburner #5567, Walnut Hollow Cone Point #5596, Walnut Hollow Double Recipe Box #14280P, Walnut Hollow Oil Color Pencils, Delta Ceramcoat Glaze Base, Delta Ceramcoat Matte Interior Spray Varnish, Decoupage Medium, Delta Ceramcoat Acrylic Paints, Fiskars Victorian Paper Edgers.

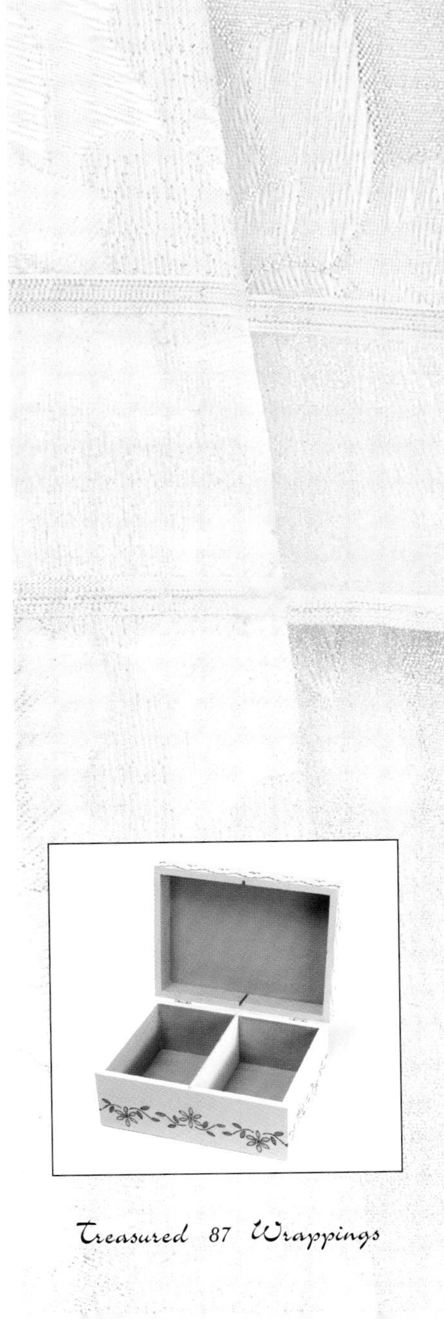

Courtesy of American Traditional Stencils

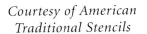

Vicki's Advanced Project

Toy Box

The "Toy Box" would be wonderful for holding that new baby gift, kids' gifts, or filled with CDs for anyone, since we're all "kids at heart."

Instructions:

Patterns on page 91-93

1. Seal the paper maché box and lid with two coats of spray varnish, letting it dry between coats.

2. Using the flat shader brush, basecoat the box and lid with two coats of Old Parchment paint, allowing it dry between coats.

3. Sand the wooden block if necessary. Basecoat it with two coats of Eggshell White paint, allowing it to dry between coats.

4. Transfer the patterns on the wooden block first. The slash marks are for your shading reference and shouldn't be transferred. Doing one side of the block at a time, lay a pattern on the side of the block and secure with small pieces of tape. Slide the transfer paper under the pattern, graphite side down, and go over the design with a ballpoint pen. Transfer "A" on the front, "B" on the right, "C" on the top, and "D" on the left. Set aside.

5. Lay the boat/yoyo pattern on the side of the box and secure it with small pieces of tape. Slide the transfer paper under the pattern, graphite side down, and go over the main lines of the design with a ballpoint pen. Don't transfer any details at this time. Move the pattern to another section of the box and repeat two times, going all around the box.

6. Transfer the lid pattern in the same way. Don't transfer the stripe or the fringes.

7. Basecoating: Basecoat using the appropriate brush for the area. Apply at least two coats of paint to prevent the bottom surface from showing through. Allow the paint to dry completely between coats. After the base coat on each segment of the design is dry, transfer the detail lines. After transferring the stripe on the lid, tape it off to achieve a straight edge while painting. *Hint: When painting an area that you have taped off, paint the original basecoat color first and allow to dry, then change to the color indicated. In this way, if the paint bleeds slightly under the tape, it will bleed the basecoat color and not the top color.* When the paint is almost dry, remove the tape slowly and carefully.

- All blocks - Eggshell White. After transferring the letters and lines, do the letters in Midnight Blue, the line around "A" in Moroccan Red, the line around "B" in Dark Foliage Green, and the line around "C" in Blue Storm.
- Sailboat - sail in Eggshell White, flag in Moroccan Red, boat in Blue Storm
- Yoyo - Alpine Green
- Jacks - Rain Grey
- Ball - Moroccan Red
- Fringed blanket - Midnight Blue. After transferring and taping the stripe, paint the stripe Moroccan Red.

8. Shading: Refer to the original pattern and shade the areas on each segment of the design indicated by slash marks. Use the appropriate angle shader

Materials:

8" hexagon paper maché box
2" wood block
8" jointed wooly bear
Matte interior spray varnish
Acrylic paint: Old Parchment, Brown Velvet, Midnight Blue, Alpine Green, Rain Grey, Dark Foliage Green, Eggshell White, Blue Storm, Moroccan Red
Black Identi-Pen
Brushes:
#6 filbert
#3 round
#12 flat shader
#10 liner
1/4" angle shader
3/8"angle shader
Graphite transfer paper
Ballpoint pen
Glue gun
Tape
Fine grit sandpaper
1 yard 3/4"-wide ribbon
Cheek blush
Paper towels

brush for straight edges or the filbert brush for the curved edges to fit the area you are shading. To achieve soft blended shading, dip your brush in water, blot it once on a paper towel (leaving some water in the brush), dip one side of the brush in paint (on an angle brush, dip the longer pointed side), stroke the brush once on a palette, then stroke it on the design. *Hint: After the shading is dry, you can shade a second time for a softer appearance.*

- All blocks - Brown Velvet
- Sailboat - sail in Rain Grey, flag in Brown Velvet
- Yoyo - Dark Foliage Green
- Jacks - Brown Velvet
- Ball - Brown Velvet
- Fringed blanket - Shade all the way around the outside of the blanket with Brown Velvet. Let dry, then refer to the original pattern and use a liner brush to paint the fringe with Midnight Blue. Let dry. Paint Moroccan Red fringe interspersed with the Midnight Blue fringe. Let dry.

9. Highlighting: Use the appropriate brush to fit the area you are highlighting. Don't add water to the brush. Dab paint in Eggshell White and stroke it across the paper towel until it's almost dry, then stroke on the design.

- Boat - from the bottom right toward the center
- Yoyo - across the center area on each section
- Jacks - each rounded end
- Ball - slightly below the center toward the right

10. Use the wide tip of the Identi-Pen to line the center pole on the sailboat, yoyo string, and across the middle of the yoyo. Use the small tip to outline all other segments of the design.

11. Shade each side of the box and lid seams with Brown Velvet. Let dry.

12. Apply two light coats of spray varnish to the entire box, lid, and block to set the ink, letting dry between coats.

13. Apply blush to the bear's cheeks. Tie the ribbon in a bow around its neck. Hold the bear on a counter in a sitting position and use the glue gun to attach its belly, right leg, and left paw to the wooden block. Also glue the right paw to the side of the snout. Then glue the bear with the block to the top of the lid.

The following products were used for this project: Brown Wooly Bear by Pacific Craft, Delta Ceramcoat Matte Interior Spray Varnish, Delta Ceramcoat Acrylic Paints, Sakura Identi-Pen, Robert Simmons Brushes.

pattern for around the box

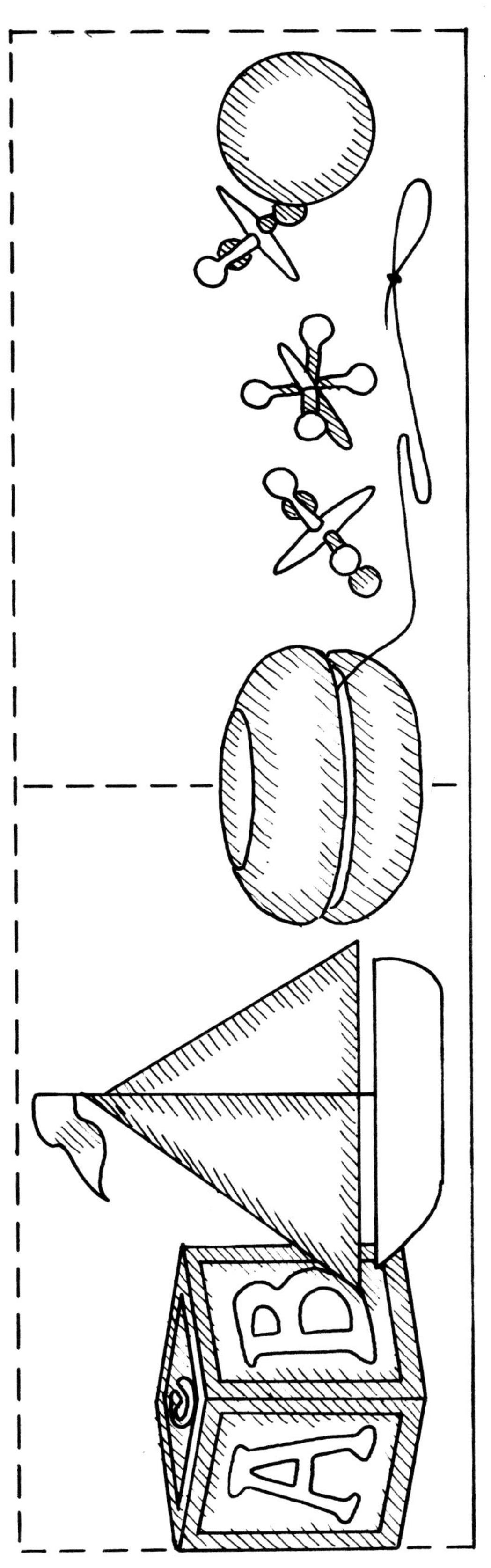

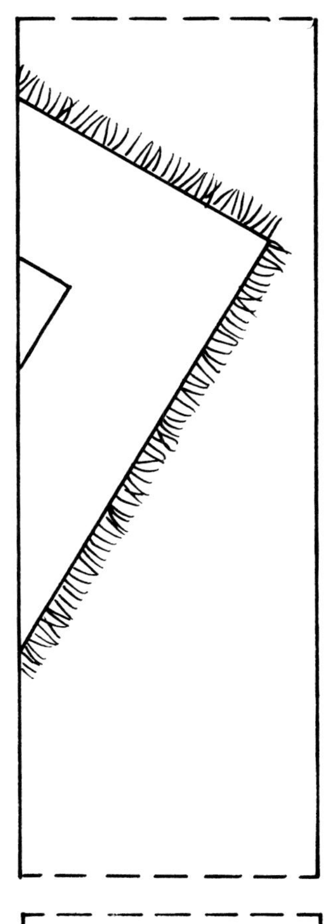

right front/back lid

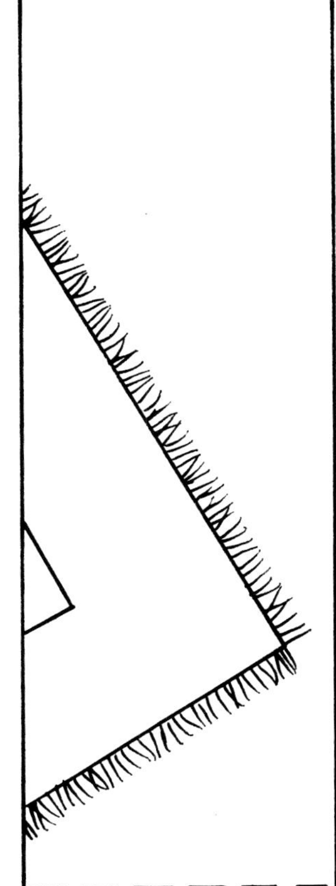

left front/back lid

pattern for wooden block

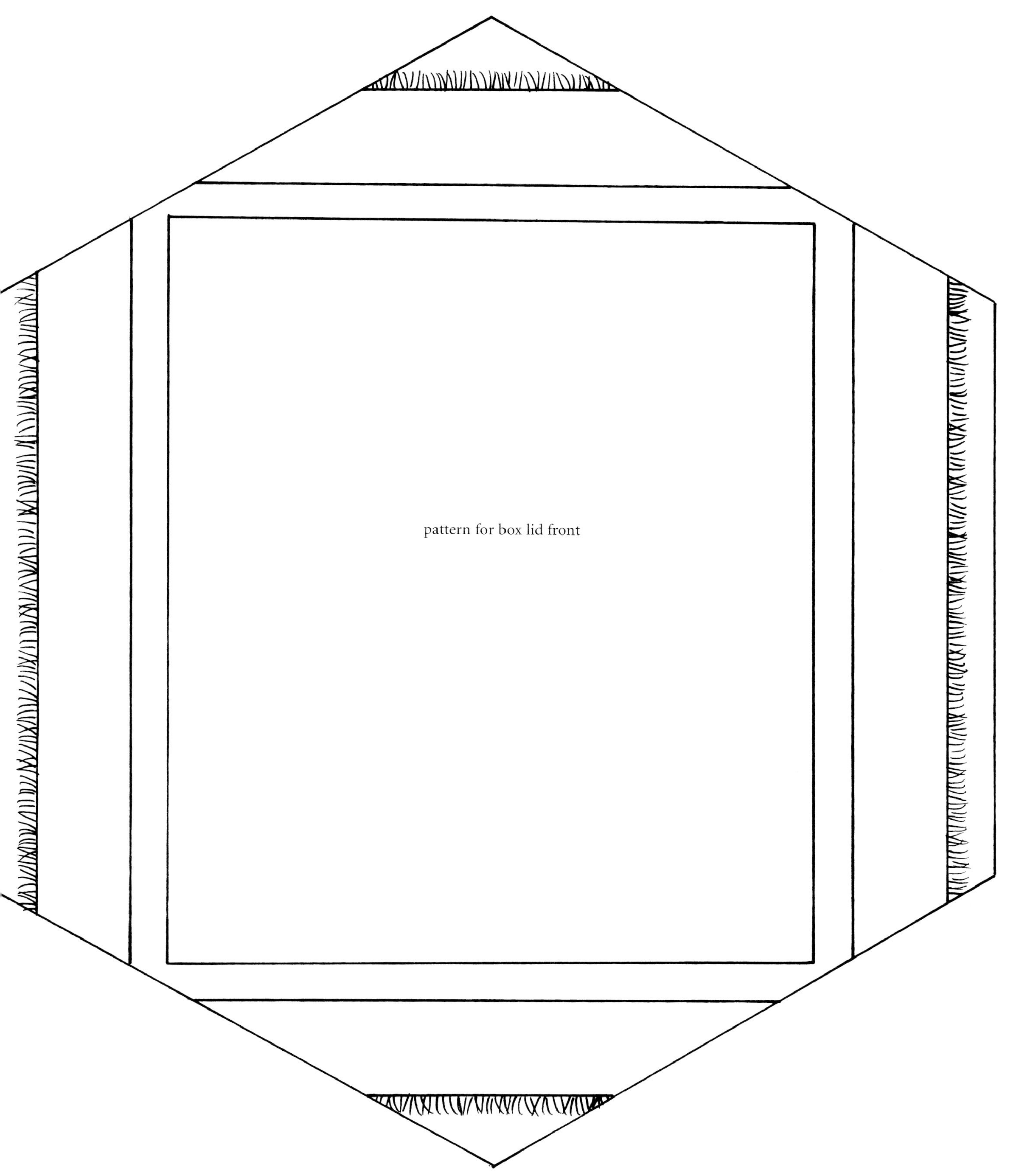
pattern for box lid front

Lisa Shepard

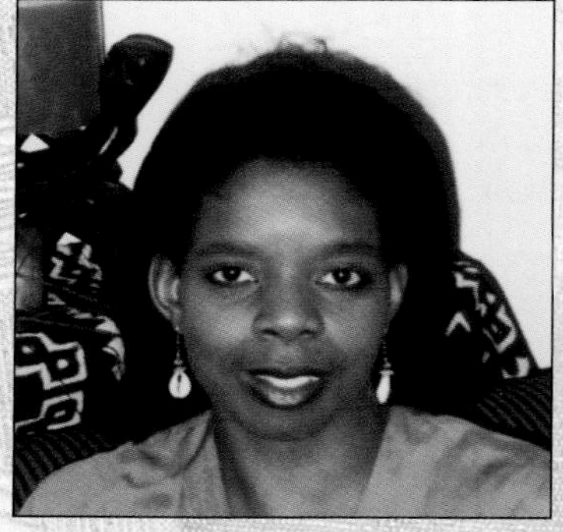

Lisa Shepard is a writer and designer based in New Jersey. A graduate of the Fashion Institute of Technology in New York City, she holds a bachelor's degree in marketing as well as an associate degree in communications. In her book, African Accents: Fabrics and Crafts to Decorate Your Home, *Lisa shares her combined passions for sewing, creative home decor, and African art. In addition to fabric collecting, she also enjoys travel, natural health, and yoga.*

Distressed Craft Paper Gift Bag

This easy and exotic looking gift bag is designed to simulate beaten bark cloth, a fiber art found in several ancient African cultures. The original techniques involved the pounding of raffia and similar plant fibers into thin, uniform textiles which were then painted, stamped, embroidered, or otherwise embellished. Try this version in animal print craft paper, distressed to give it a "beaten" look, then trimmed with raffia ties and beads.

For extra memory mileage, use trims that can be converted into a pendant, earrings, or a pin with the simple addition of jewelry findings.

Instructions:

1. To distress the craft paper, *lightly* mist the paper with water using a spray bottle. Let it sit for a minute to absorb into the paper. Begin crumpling the paper evenly all over, working gently to avoid tearing the paper. Crumple until the entire piece is balled up, then unravel the piece and flatten it out.

2. Use an iron to dry the paper. Any rips in the paper can be patched with strips of paper and fusible tape; the texture and print will camouflage the repairs. Press down lightly on the paper to set the creases (pressing too heavily will reduce the creased texture).

3. Fold in the two sides toward the center, overlapping the ends 1". Place fusible hem tape between the overlapping edges and fuse.

4. Fold up 3/4" on the bottom edge of the bag. Tuck in the corners for a neat finish and fuse.

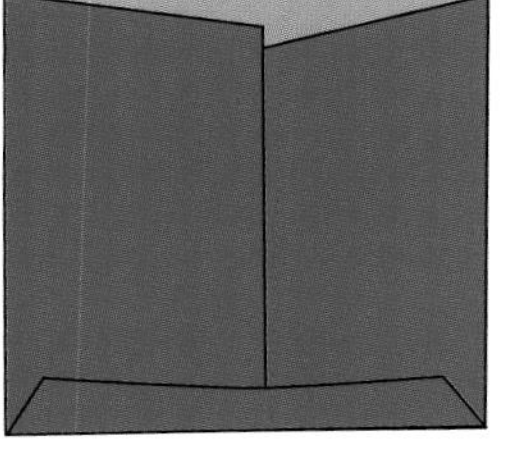

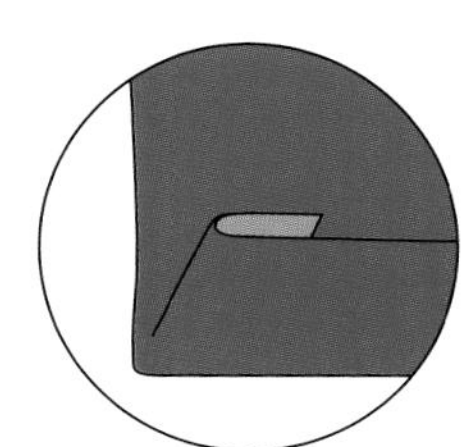

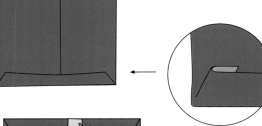

5. Fold in the upper corners of the bag and fold the flap down, envelope style. Secure with a small piece of transparent tape if necessary. Tie loose raffia fibers around the package. Slip assorted trims on the raffia and knot the ends to secure.

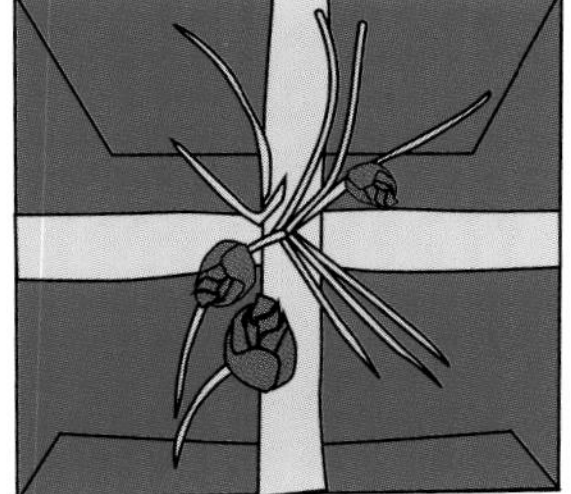

The following products were used for this project: Craft Paper and Raffia Ties by Loose Ends, Trims by One World Button Supply Co., Stitch Witchery Fusible Hem Tape by HTC-Handler Textile Corp.

Materials:

to make a bag approx. 7" x 8"

Animal print craft paper, 20" x 20"
Loose strands of raffia in two coordinating colors
Beads, buttons, cowrie shells (or embellishments of choice)
Fusible web tape
Spray bottle
Iron

Lisa's Intermediate Project

Fabric Ribbon Mini Gift Basket

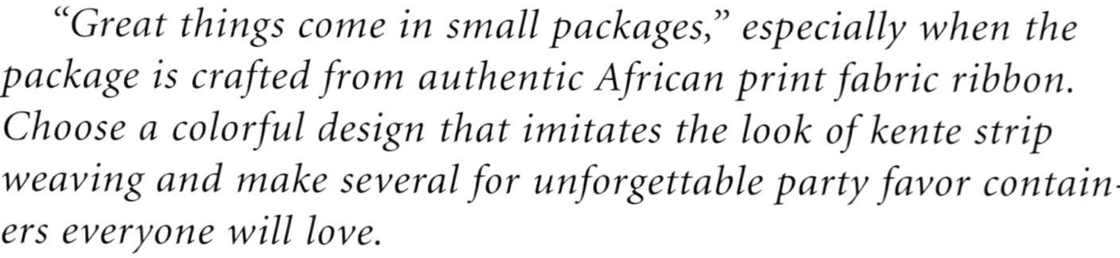

"Great things come in small packages," especially when the package is crafted from authentic African print fabric ribbon. Choose a colorful design that imitates the look of kente strip weaving and make several for unforgettable party favor containers everyone will love.

Place weights inside the baskets and use them as bases for balloon centerpieces. They're also small enough to be used as unique Christmas tree ornaments. They even make a great presentation in formal dining settings - fill each with a small surprise, add a gift tag, and use them in lieu of place cards.

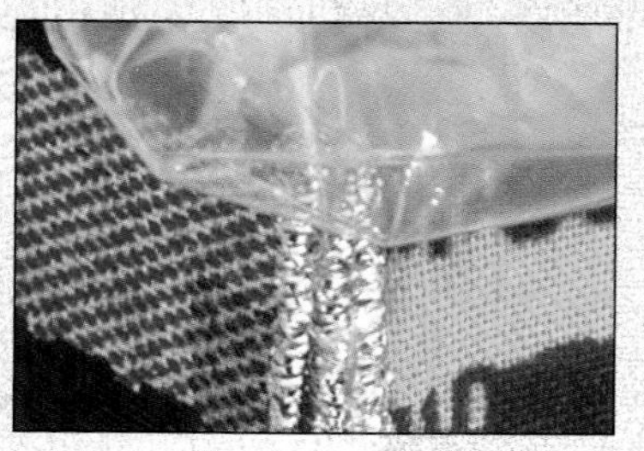

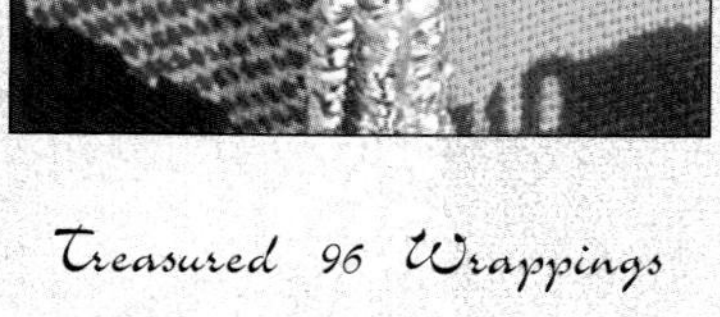

Instructions:

1. Cut a 24" length of fabric ribbon. Place the craft backing against the wrong side of the ribbon so the edges of the craft backing don't extend beyond the edges of the ribbon. Cut the ribbon in half to form two 12" pieces.

2. Fold up 2-1/2" on each end, then fold again to form a U shape. Try to avoid putting a sharp crease in the wire, instead bending it so it remains slightly rounded. This will prevent the wire from breaking.

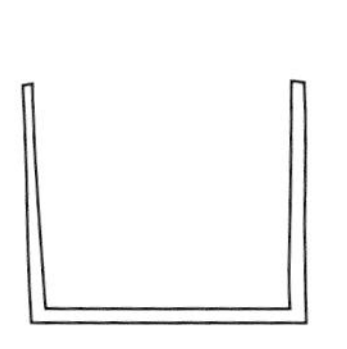

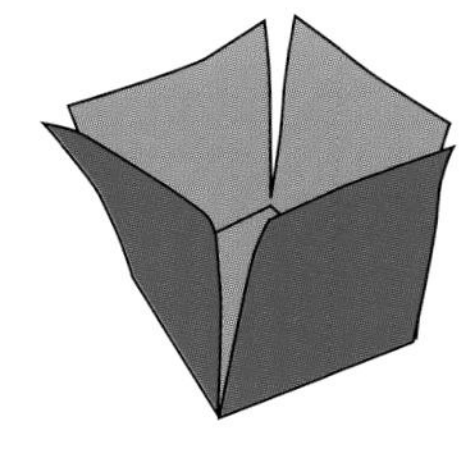

3. Hot glue the inside flaps in place. Position one U shape inside the other to form a box; glue the bottoms together. Then glue the corners from the inside so any excess glue won't show on the right side.

4. Cut a 7" length of ribbon for the basket handle. Make lengthwise pleats in the center and secure the pleats with a small amount of glue. Position the ends of the handle inside the basket so the raw edge of the handle is 1" down from the top of the basket. Glue the handle in place.

5. Wrap the gift or party favor in a piece of cellophane measuring approximately 14" square. Place the gift inside the basket and arrange the gathered cellophane to extend from both sides of the handle. Tie narrow satin ribbons to the handle.

The following products were used in this project: African Fabric Ribbon by AfriCraft, Fusible Craft Backing by HTC-Handler Textile Corp.

Materials:

1 yard wire edge African fabric ribbon, 2-1/2"-wide
24" fusible craft backing, 2-1/4"-wide
Coordinating cellophane
Coordinating ribbon, 3/8"-wide

Lisa's Advanced Project

Duffel Bag & Reusable Gift Tag

This duffel is perfect to wrap a travel-related gift for people on the go! The gift tag also does double duty, since it can be used by the recipient as a photo frame key tag or luggage I.D. tag. It's done in an imported African fabric that resembles traditional kente cloth, but is machine woven for greater durability for fashion accessories and home dec applications.

Instructions:

1. Cut the fabric and interfacing to 12" long x 13" wide. Fuse the interfacing to the wrong side of the fabric. Finish the upper edge with a serger or zigzag stitch.

2. Sew a row of gathering stitches along the bottom edge. With right sides together, stitch a 1/2" lengthwise seam. Press open.

3. To make the drawstring casing at the top, turn in 1" and stitch close to the serged edge. Stitch again 1/2" and 5/8" from the folded edge. Break the stitching of the lengthwise seam between the last two rows of the casing stitching. Insert the drawstring through this opening, using a safety pin. Pull the string through the casing so the ends are even. Slip the bead over the ends of both strings and slide it to the top edge of the bag. Pin the ends to the lower edge of the bag.

4. Fuse a piece of interfacing to a piece of fabric at least 5" square. From the fused piece, cut a 4 -1/2" circle for the bottom of the duffel. With right sides together, pin the bottom to the duffel, drawing up the gathering stitches along the lower edge of the bag as needed. Stitch a 1/2" seam, catching in the ends of the drawstring handle.

5. To make the reusable gift tag, cut a window out of one sticky board piece to resemble a mini picture frame. Cover both sticky board pieces with fabric. On the cutout piece, clip the inner fabric and fold it through the opening to the inside. Fold the thin cording in half and position the ends along the edge of the board pieces. Glue the two fabric-covered sticky board pieces wrong sides together along three sides, including the cording ends. Write the gift greeting on a small piece of paper and insert it in the tag, along with the clear acetate photo protector. Add the spring ring to the cording loop and slip the ring on the drawstring above the bead.

The following products were used for this project: African Fabric by Homeland Authentics, Fusible Interfacing by HTC-Handler Textile Corp., Sticky-Back Mounting Board by Crescent.

Materials:

1/2 yard African woven kente fabric
1/2 yard woven fusible interfacing
1-1/4 yard durable cording (for drawstring handle)
1 wooden bead (hole large enough for two thicknesses of cording to pass through)
2 pieces sticky-back mounting board, 2" x 1-3/4"
Spring key ring
4" length of thin cording (to attach gift tag)
Clear acetate photo protector, 1" x 1-1/2"

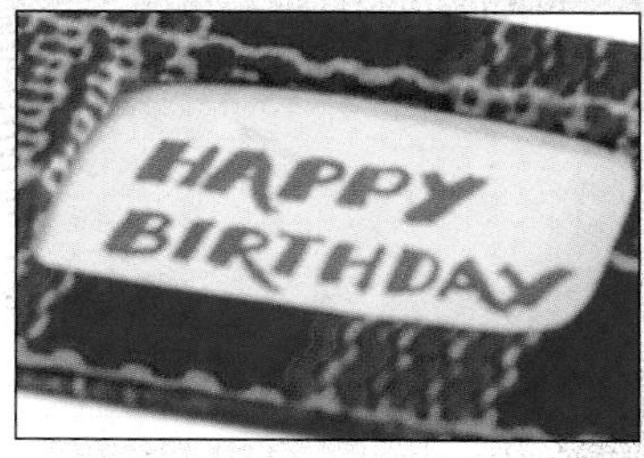

Impressed Velvet Keepsake Box

Brenda's Beginner Project

Brenda L. Spitzer

Brenda developed a love for arts and crafts at an early age when her mother taught her to paint clay pots, her grandmother taught her embroidery, and her father taught her wax resist egg decorating. Now she enjoys passing the family crafting traditions on to her three children and one grandchild.

No sewing is required to create this elegant little box. Floral and butterfly motifs are impressed into velvet which is then used to cover a paper maché base. Glass beads and a jacquard lining add a finishing touch.

Instructions:

1. Place three lace flowers and three lace butterflies on the piece of sheet cork and trace around them with the water-soluble marking pencil. Remove the lace shapes and place the cork on the cutting mat. Cut out the traced shapes using the razor knife. Set aside.

2. For the outside of the box and lid, cut the following pieces of cranberry velvet:
(1) 10" x 3-1/4"
(2) 3-3/4" x 3-1/4"
(1) 3-1/2" x 3-1/2"
(1) 12-1/4" x 1-1/4"

3. For the lining of the box and lid, cut the following pieces of ivory jacquard:
(1) 8-1/2" x 3"
(2) 3-1/4" x 3"
(1) 4-1/2" x 3-1/4"
(2) 3-1/4" x 1"

4. To impress on the velvet, fill your iron with distilled water and preheat to a medium setting. Fold a hand towel in half and place it on a hard surface. Set the 12-1/4" x 1-1/4" piece of velvet aside. Working with one piece of velvet at a time, place the remaining pieces of velvet with right sides up on the towel. Place the lace butterfly and flower shapes randomly on the velvet. Spray lightly with water and cover the shapes with their appropriate cork template. Wet a second hand towel with water and wring it out. Place the wet towel over the cork, lace, velvet, and bottom towel. Place the iron over the cork template and press down with a steady firm pressure for 15 seconds. Remove the top towel and gently lift the cork template and lace shape to check the impression. If more impression is desired, repeat the pressing process for an additional ten seconds. Once the desired impression is achieved, remove the towel, cork templates, and lace. Place the 12-1/4" x 1- 1/4" piece of velvet on the towel. Center the loop braid lengthwise on the velvet, spray lightly with water, cover with a damp towel, and impress as above.

5. Use the beading needle and coordinating thread to stitch three crystal glass beads to the center of each impressed flower. Stitch a row of five amethyst glass pebble beads to the body of each impressed butterfly.

6. To line the lid, use Fabri-Tac to glue the two 3-1/4" x 1" pieces of ivory lining in place on opposite sides inside the rim. Wrap and glue the edge of the lining fabric over the bottom edge of the rim. Turn under 1/4" and glue both long edges of the 4-1/2" x 3-1/4" piece of lining fabric. Glue in place inside the lid, covering the top and remaining sides. Wrap and glue the edges over the bottom of the rim.

7. To cover the lid, glue the 3-1/2" x 3-1/2" piece of velvet on the top of the lid. Turn under 1/4" and glue both long edges of the 12-1/4" x 1-1/4" velvet

Materials:

to make a 3-1/4" square box

Paper maché box,
2-3/4" wide x 3-1/4" high
1/6 yard cranberry velvet
1/6 yard ivory jacquard
Fabri-Tac Permanent Adhesive
3 lace butterflies
7 lace flowers (cut from lace garland)
White loop braid
6" x 6" natural cork sheet
12" x 18" cutting mat
15 amethyst pebble beads
21 crystal glass beads
Water-soluble marking pencil
2 terry cloth hand towels
Razor knife
Scissors
Beading needle
Matching thread
Iron

piece. Turn under 1/4" and glue one end of the strip. Beginning with the raw end of the strip, glue it in place around the rim of the lid, stretching as you go. Finish the lid by gluing the folded end over the raw end.

8. Cover the box by using Fabri-Tac to glue the two 3-3/4" x 3-1/4" pieces of velvet in place on opposite sides of the outside of the box. Fold and glue the side and bottom edges of velvet over the sides and bottom of the box. Wrap and glue the top edges of velvet over the top edges of the box. Turn under 1/4" and glue both long edges of the 10" x 3-1/4" piece of velvet. Glue in place on the outside of the box, covering the bottom and remaining sides. Wrap and glue the top edges of the velvet over the top edges of the box.

9. Line the box by using Fabri-Tac to glue the two 3-1/4" x 3" pieces of ivory jacquard inside the box on opposite sides. Fold the top edges of the lining down and glue to the velvet on the inside of the box. Turn under 1/4" and glue both long edges of the 8-1/2" x 3" lining piece. Glue it in place inside the box, covering the bottom and remaining sides. Fold under and glue the top edges of the lining to the velvet on the inside of the box.

The following products were used for this project: Fidelio Cranberry Velvet by J.B. Martin, Cloud 9 Ivory Jacquard by Logantex, Inc., Fabri-Tac Permanent Adhesive by Beacon, Lace Butterflies #MP5434-12 and Lace Flower Garland #VP5900-12 by Modern Romance, Inc., White Loop Braid #535 by Wrights, Handi Cork Natural Cork Sheet by Universal Cork, Inc., Amethyst Pebble Beads #05202 and Crystal Glass Beads # 60161 by Mill Hill.

Hexagonal Felt Keepsake Box

Brenda's Intermediate Project

This box is made with stiffened felt. I added texture by impressing a design into the felt, then sponge painted it and trimmed it with glass beads, organza ribbon, and metallic thread.

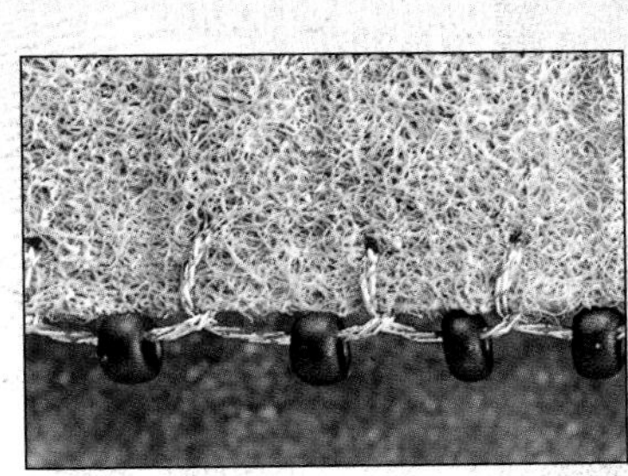

Materials:

to make a 4" x 3" box

12" x 18" sheet white felt
Acrylic paints: Cornsilk Yellow, Truly Teal
Clear glaze base
Pearl luster medium
Metallic embroidery thread
9mm Mint Green organza ribbon embroidery floss
Matching sewing thread
27 semiprecious stone beads, 4.5mm
Box of tiny antique glass beads
Water-soluble marking pencil
6 jumbo metal paper clips
Small sea silk sponge
Scissors
Embroidery needle, size 9
Chenille needle, size 24
Iron
Terry cloth hand towel
Press cloth

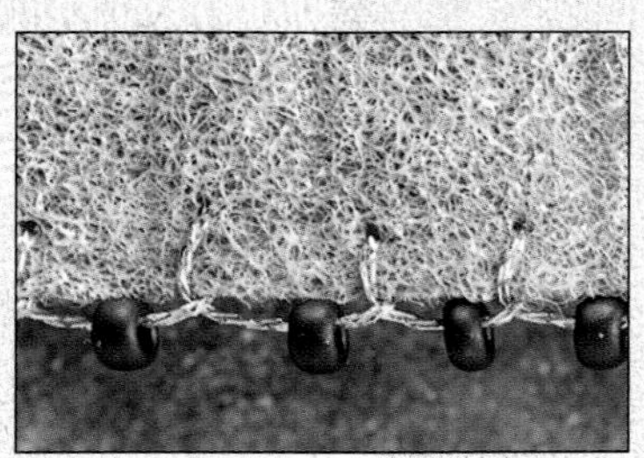

Instructions:

Patterns on page 106

1. Pin the box and lid patterns on the white felt. Use the marking pencil to trace around the patterns, then cut them out.

2. Preheat the iron to a medium setting. Fold the towel in half and place it on a hard surface. Place the felt lid piece on the towel. Work with two of the six sides of the lid at a time. Arrange three evenly spaced paper clips vertically on each side. Line up the cut ends of the paper clips with the bottom edge of the felt and spray lightly with water. Cover with a damp press cloth. With firm pressure, press the paper clips into the felt for 15 seconds. Allow to cool. Remove the press cloth and paper clips. Repeat the impressions on the remaining sides. Set the lid aside. Place the felt box piece on the towel. Work with one of the six sides at a time. Arrange three evenly spaced paper clips vertically on each side, lining up the cut ends of the paper clips with the fold line for the bottom of the box. Impress as above.

3. To sponge paint the box and lid, mix a base coat of one part Teal acrylic paint with one part clear glaze base. Place the felt pieces with the impressed sides up on the work surface. Moisten the sea sponge with water and wring it out. Dip the sponge into the paint/glaze mixture and blot it lightly on a paper towel. Sponge the paint on the felt using a light pouncing movement. Alternate the direction of the sponge as you work. Turn the felt over and sponge paint the back. Let dry. Mix one part Yellow acrylic paint, one part clear glaze base, and one part Pearl luster medium. Place the felt pieces with the impressed sides up on the work surface. Repeat the sponge painting process over the base color, applying one coat on the box base and two coats on the lid. Allow to dry between coats.

4. For the three ribbon embroidery flowers, press the creases out of the 9mm organza ribbon with a low temperature iron. Pull approximately 2" of floss through the eye of the chenille needle and insert the point of the needle through this 2" section approximately 3/4" from the end. Tug at the floss until it locks around the eye of the needle. Knot the bottom end of the floss and stitch three loop stitch flowers with five petals each to the top of the lid where indicated on the pattern. Stitch each petal by bringing the needle and floss up through the felt. Form a smooth loop by bringing the floss toward you and over your finger. Insert the needle through both the floss and felt at a point directly behind the starting point. Pull the floss through to form a petal approximately 1/2" long. Repeat for the remaining petals.

5. On the lid, use an embroidery needle to stitch five tiny antique glass beads near the base of each flower petal. Stitch one semiprecious stone to the center of each flower and one 3/8" from each corner of the lid. On the box, stitch three semiprecious stones to each side within the arches of the impressed paper clips.

6. Thread the embroidery needle with a single strand of metallic thread knotted at the bottom. Fold the six sides of the box up with right sides out. Working with two sides at a time, connect the sides with a figure 8 stitch by bringing the needle from the inside to the outside at one lower corner of a box side. Pull the thread through and insert the needle under the adjoining side, thus forming a figure 8. Repeat for the remaining sides.

7. Connect all the sides of the lid with the figure 8 stitch as above. Finish the bottom edge of the lid with a beaded blanket stitch. To begin the beaded blanket stitch, bring the needle from the back to the front of the felt approximately 1/8" from the bottom edge at point A. Bring the needle over the edge to the back and again through to the front at point A, forming a loop over the edge. Pull the thread securely. Run the needle under the loop from right to left. Run the needle through a tiny antique glass bead, pulling the bead to the bottom. Insert the needle from the front to the back of the felt at point B, approximately 1/8" from the edge and 3/8" from point A. Keep the thread behind the needle and pull securely. Repeat this stitch around the entire edge of the lid.

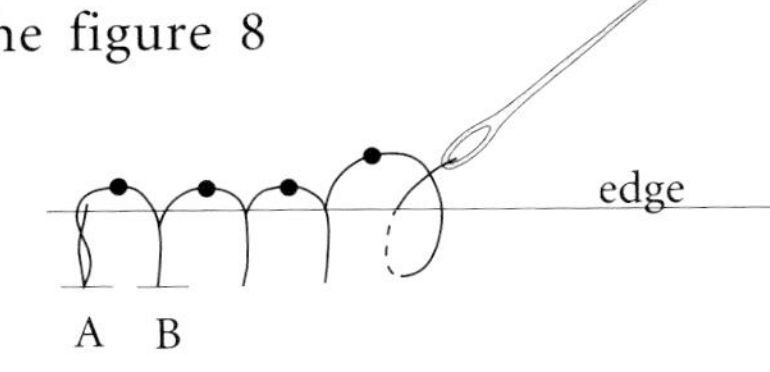

The following products were used for this project: White Eazy Felt #0650 by CPE, Delta Ceramcoat Acrylic Paints, Delta Faux Finish Clear Glaze Base, Delta Pearl Luster Medium, Organza Ribbon Embroidery Floss by Bucilla, Semiprecious Stone Beads #5-78 by Gick Beads/Creative Beginnings, Antique Glass Beads #03028 by Mill Hill.

Knot the end of the thread and insert the needle at A. Pull the thread through and bring it around the edge of Side 1 to the inside of Side 2. Insert the needle at B and pull it through. Bring the thread around the edge of Side 2 to the inside of Side 1. Insert the needle at C. Continue stitching until you reach the top, then knot the thread on the inside and run the needle under the last two stitches.

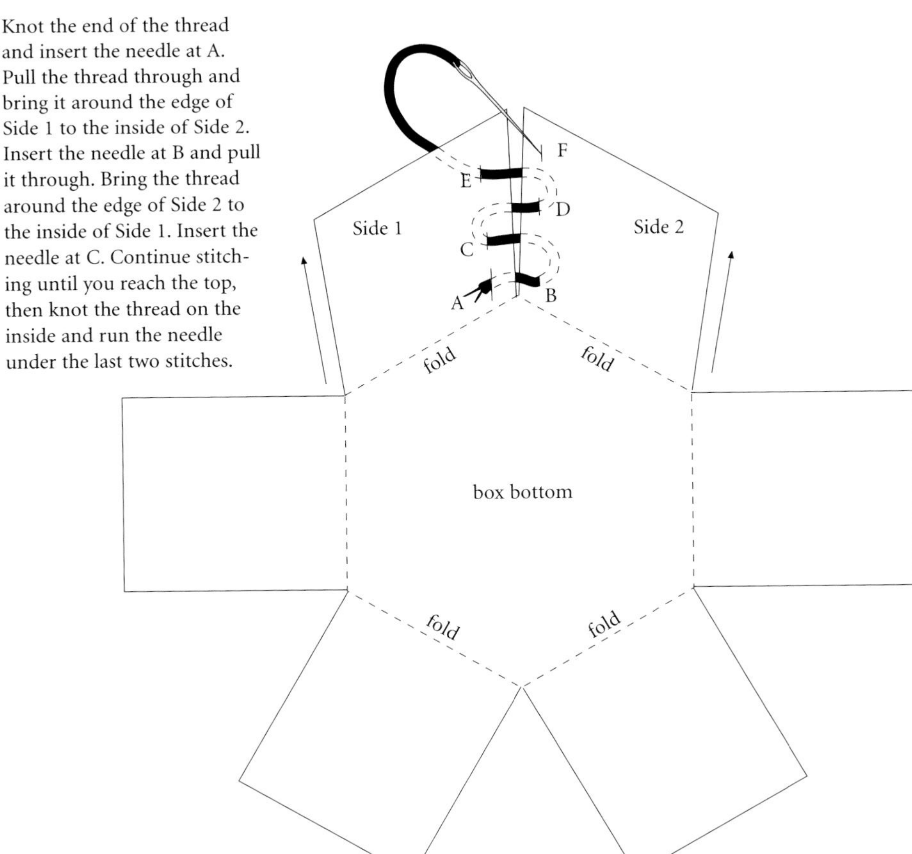

pattern for box

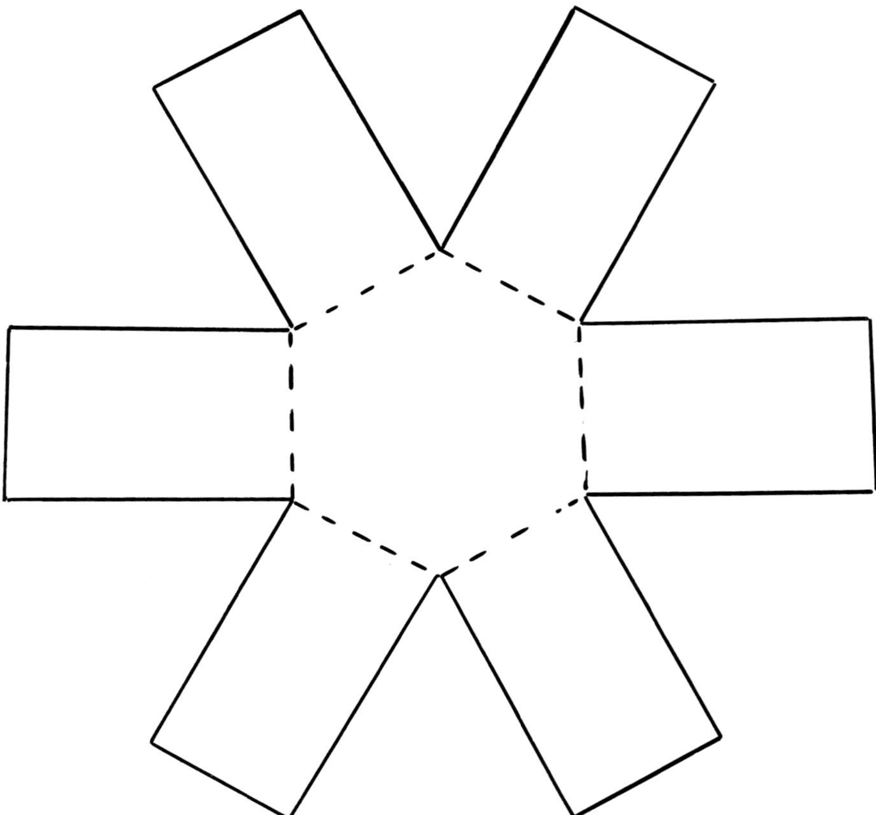

Enlarge 200%

pattern for lid

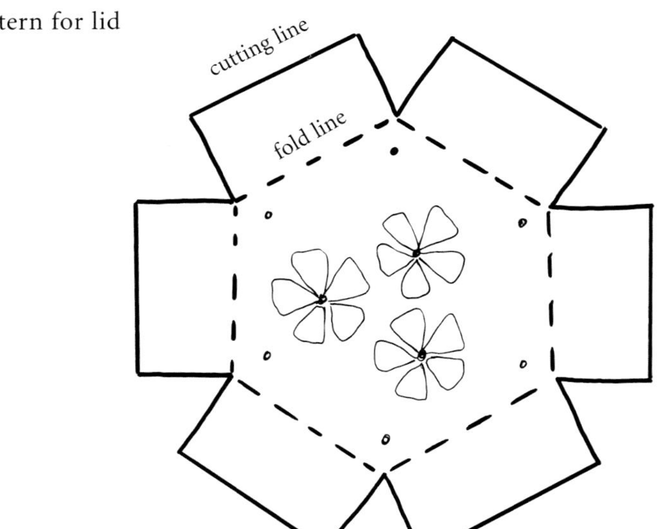

Enlarge 200%

Organza Embroidered Bag

Brenda's Advanced Project

Chiffon embroidered with organza flowers and accented with glass beads is layered over a sparkling jacquard. The layers are sewn together to construct a simple bag and tie.

Materials:

to make a 11" x 9" bag

2/3 yard periwinkle poly chiffon, 44"-wide
1/2 yard lavender polyester, 44"-wide
Matching thread
9mm organza ribbon embroidery floss: 2 spools Pink, 2 spools Lt. Mauve, 2 spools Gold, 2 spools Mint Green
5mm organza ribbon embroidery floss: Light Blue, Purple
Glass beads:
5 each size 5/0 White Frosted and Blue
5 green assorted sizes green semiprecious stone beads
16 size 8/0 Ceylon Snowflake
Water-soluble marking pencil
Scissors
Chenille needle, size 24
Embroidery needle, size 9
Masking tape
Needlework hoop or frame
Iron
Sewing machine

Instructions:

1. Cut a piece of chiffon 18" x 24". Use the marking pencil to mark the placement of the five-petal flowers and the cross-stitch flowers (refer to the photo or place as desired). Stretch the fabric taut in a needlework frame or hoop.

2. To make the five-petal ribbon flowers, first iron the creases out of all the 9mm ribbon floss and cut all colors in lengths of approximately 25". To begin ribbon embroidery, pull approximately 2" of ribbon floss through the eye of the chenille needle. Insert the needle through this 2" section about 3/4" from the end. Tug at the long section of floss until it locks around the eye of the needle. Knot the bottom end of the floss. Use Gold, Pink, and Lt. Mauve floss to embroider the five-petal flowers. Use Mint Green floss for the leaves. Each petal and leaf is stitched as follows: Bring the needle up from the back to the front at point A. Form a loop, holding the floss with your fingers so it doesn't twist. Insert the needle and pull the floss down through the fabric at point B. Holding the loop between your finger and thumb, bring the needle up at point C and down at D to hold the top of the petal or leaf in place. Repeat for the remaining petals.

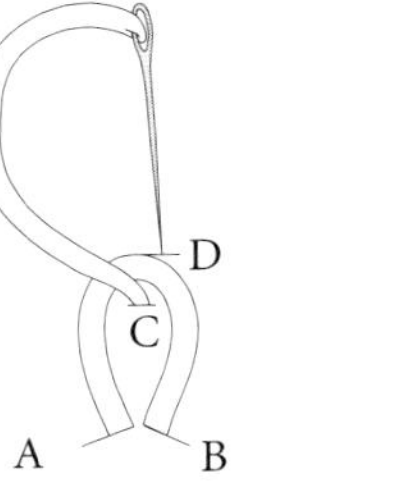

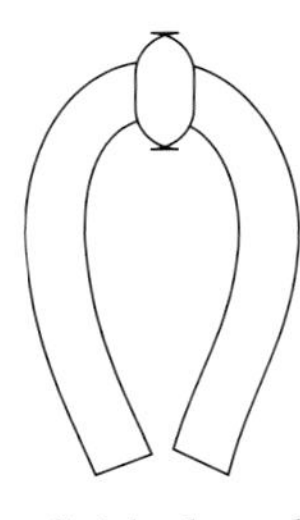
finished petal

finished flower

3. To make the cross-stitch flowers, first iron the creases out of all the 5mm ribbon floss. Use Light Blue and Purple floss to embroider cross-stitch flowers as follows: Thread the chenille needle with floss. Bring the needle up from the back to the front at point A. Insert the needle and pull the floss down through the fabric at point B. Bring the needle up at point C and down at D.

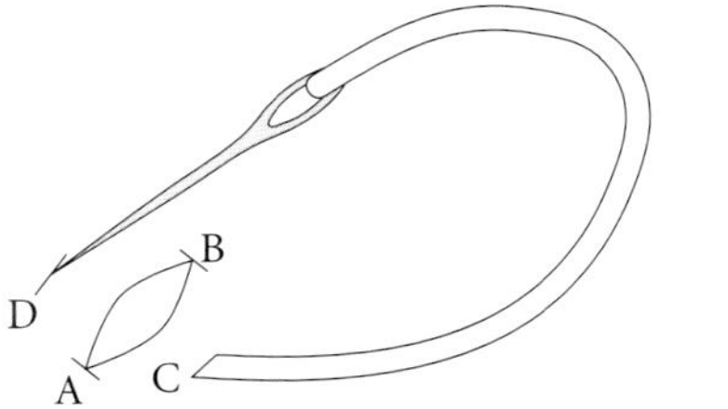

finished flower

4. Beading - Use the embroidery needle to stitch Ceylon Snowflake beads to the center of each cross-stitch flower. Stitch White Frosted beads to the center of the Lt. Mauve five-petal flowers; Blue beads to the Pink five-petal flowers, and Green beads to the Gold five-petal flowers.

5. Assembling the bag - Cut the embroidered chiffon to 12" x 20". Cut two pieces of jacquard 12" x 20". Fold each piece of fabric in half with right sides together to form a 12" x 10" rectangle. Use a sewing machine to sew pouches by stitching the side and bottom edges with a 1/2" seam. Trim the corners. Turn the chiffon and one jacquard pouch right side out. Press the seams with a low temperature iron. Place the jacquard pouch inside the chiffon pouch with the top edges lined up. Hand baste the top edges together. For the lining, insert this pair of pouches in the second jacquard pouch with right sides together. Hand baste all the top edges together. Use a sewing machine to stitch the top edge with a 1/2" seam, leaving a 3" opening for turning. Turn the bag with the lining to the inside. Press the top edge with a low temperature iron. Slipstitch the opening.

6. To make the tie - Cut one piece of chiffon and two pieces of jacquard 2" x 25". Layer and pin these pieces together with the chiffon in the middle. Stitch all the edges with a 1/2" seam, leaving a 3" opening for turning. Turn right side out. Press the edges with a low temperature iron. Slipstitch the opening.

The following products were used for this project: 9mm and 5mm Organza Ribbon Embroidery Floss by Bucilla, #5-12 White Frosted Beads, #5-25 Blue Beads, #5-052 Semiprecious Stone Beads, #4-182 Ceylon Snowflake Beads by Gick Beads/Creative Beginnings.

Nancy's Beginner Project

Nancy Tribolet

Nancy has been crafting for the better part of her life, dabbling in many facets of the industry. She has developed the "Stencils by Nancy" line and teaches seminars and workshops to groups and organizations around the country.

A Gift For the Gardener

What gardener could resist this geranium bag? Stenciling transforms a plain bag into a personalized gift package for the flower lover on your gift list.

Instructions:

Patterns are on pages 112-113

1. On the back of the watercolor paper, measure and mark the dimensions shown on the pattern. As shown, this pattern requires paper 22-1/2" wide and 13-3/4" high. You can adjust the size of the bag by enlarging or reducing the dimensions. Use a ruler and pencil to mark the fold lines with a dotted line and the cutting lines with a solid line. Cut out the pattern you've drawn, using decorative edge scissors for the top edge if desired.

2. Fold the paper into the bag shape before painting to determine where to position the stencils. Make sharp creases so the fold lines will be visible on the unmarked side where you will be working.

3. To stencil, pick up a tiny bit of paint and work it on the edge of the stencil or on a palette to work the paint into the brush and to remove the excess. Apply the paint lightly, adding more coats to strengthen the color. Blend the colors softly.

4. Begin stenciling with the flower pot. First stencil Yellow Ochre all over, then stencil Paprika to achieve the color of terra cotta. Shade with Bark Brown. To add the rim line, cover the rim with the pot drop out and stencil first with Paprika, then with Bark Brown.

5. The geranium is a three-part overlay. Position the #1 overlay and stencil the leaves and stems with Christmas Green and the flowers with Christmas Red. Mark the registration points and remove the first overlay. Position #2 and stencil again with Christmas Green on the leaves and Christmas Red on the flowers. These additional coats of color will provide enough contrast to give the detail needed. Remove #2 and position #3. Stencil the final detail as above.

6. The bee is a two-part stencil. The stripes are Basic Black and Yellow Ochre (begin with a black stripe, add yellow, repeat black, etc.). The wings are Basic Black applied very lightly.

7. Add the detail with the black marker. Rather than outlining with a defined line, sketch the outline to create a softer look.

8. Stencil the word geranium with Basic Black on the side of the bag. Use masking tape or sticky notes to mask around the letters you are stenciling.

9. The subtle green and red coloration is done by "rouging." When applying the color, be very soft - it is like cleaning the brush. When you have to pick up additional paint, be very conservative.

10. To make the handle, thread beads on two pieces of wire approximately 24" long. One of the wires should be at least 40 gauge to provide stability. Twist the wires together, separating the beads and fixing them in place. Punch a hole about 1/2" from the top on each side of the bag. Thread the wire ends through the holes and twist to secure. Randomly add some shorter pieces of twisted wire to the handle to add interest. Add some curled wire to the base of the handle.

The following products were used for this project: Calligraphy Alphabet Stencil Mini by Delta, Delta Sobo Glue, Delta Stencil Creme Paints, Sakura Identi-Pen.

Materials:

Precut stencils: Calligraphy Alphabet
Stencil paint creme: Yellow Ochre, Paprika, Bark Brown, Christmas Red, Christmas Green, Basic Black
Craft glue
(6) 3/8" stencil brushes
18" x 24" cold press 140# watercolor paper
Ruler
Scissors
Decorative edge scissors (optional)
Pencil & eraser
Paper towels
Black Identi-Pen
Assorted beads
Assorted wire for handle (shown - green, gold, silver)
Hole punch
Masking tape or sticky notes

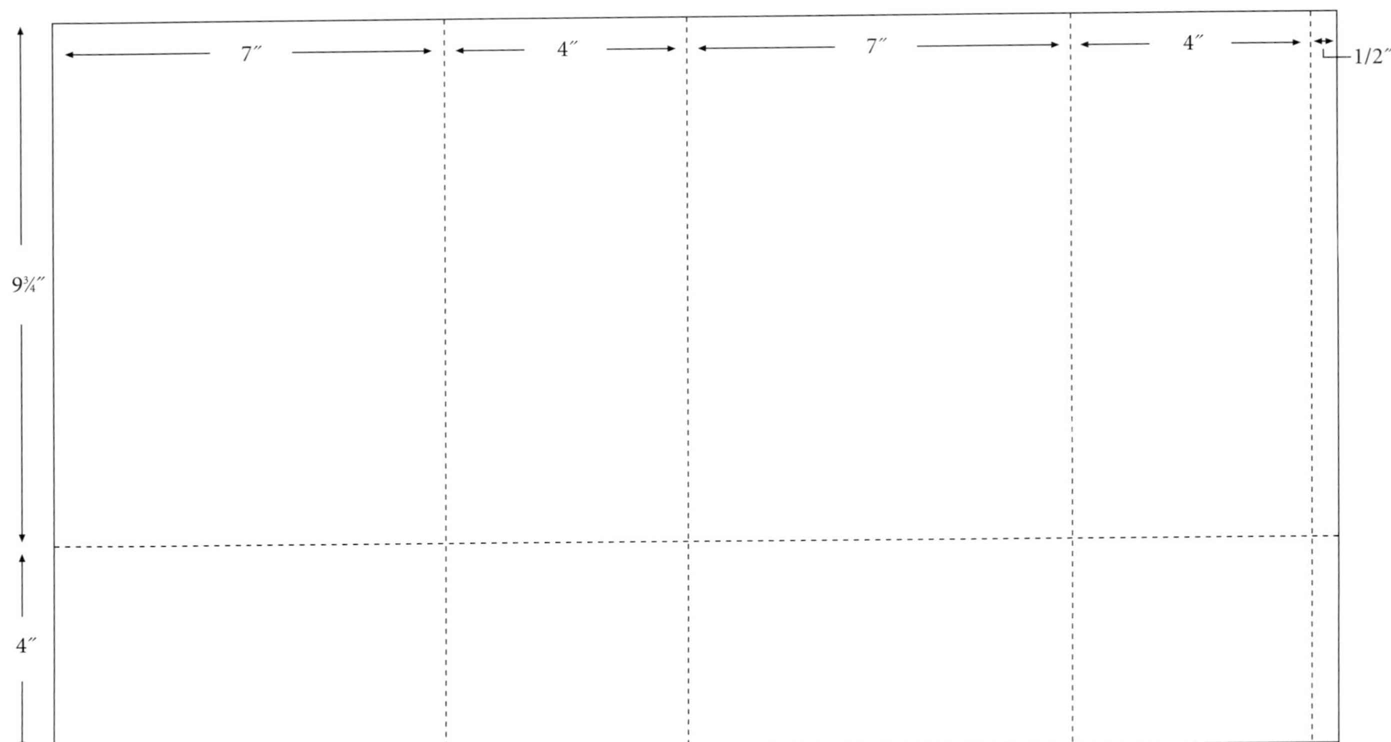

Enlarge bag pattern to dimensions shown. Solid lines are cut lines, broken lines are fold lines.

Enlarge 200%

Enlarge 200%

Enlarge flower pot 200%

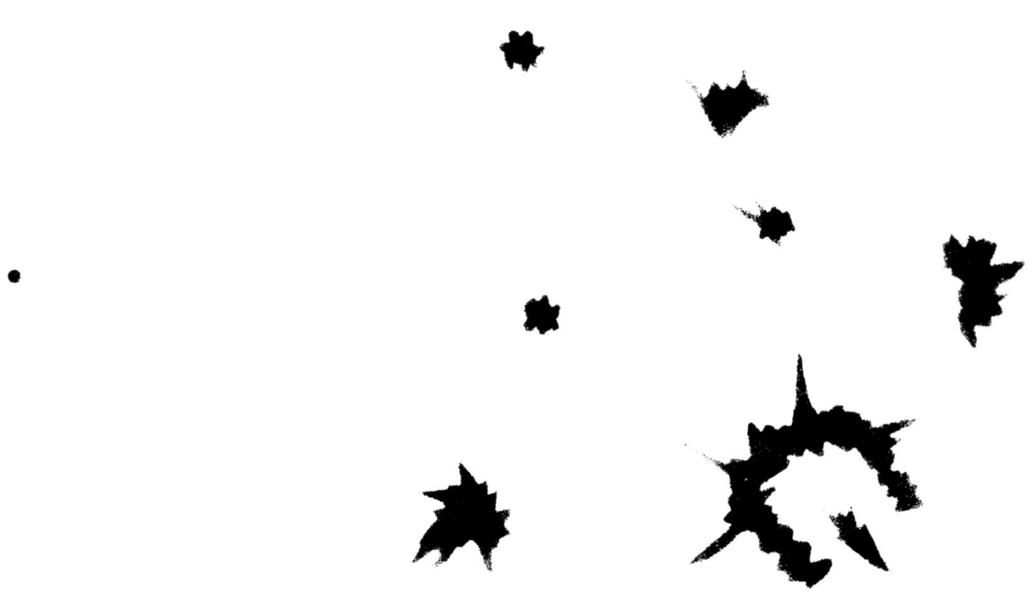

Nancy's Intermediate Project

A Father's Box

This unique domed box is perfect for a vintage photo. Choose one that will be especially meaningful to the man in your life.

Instructions:

1. Set aside the box insert and dome. Use the sponge brush to basecoat the outside of the box and lid with Chocolate Cherry acrylic paint. Basecoat the inside of the box and lid and the bottom side of the insert with Moroccan Red. You may need to apply more than one coat for good coverage. Allow to dry thoroughly.

2. On a palette, mix an equal amount of clear glaze base with Moroccan Red paint. Brush a generous coat of this mixture on the outside of the box. While the glaze mixture is still wet, lay crumpled pieces of plastic wrap diagonally over it and with a brayer (a paint bottle laid on its side works also) roll the plastic wrap against the surface. Pull it off and allow the box to dry. Repeat the process on the lid.

3. When the finish is dry, follow the manufacturer's directions and apply the gilded accents around the bottom edge of the box and around the circle opening on the lid.

4. Mist all the surfaces again with interior matte spray varnish.

5. Brush on a coat of Brown antiquing gel and wipe it off with a soft rag or paper towels.

6. Apply gloss exterior varnish to all surfaces.

7. Photocopy your favorite black and white photograph (you'll get a better copy from a color photocopier, even if the photograph is black and white). Reduce or enlarge this copy to fit in the dome opening.

8. Mist both sides of the photocopy with interior matte spray varnish.

9. Apply a coat of satin decoupage medium to the back side of the photocopy and adhere it to the insert from the lid (unpainted side). Use a brayer to press it on the lid insert, smoothing out any air pockets.

10. Tint the picture with the soft tints. Thin them with water to the point of being dirty water (it is easier to add color than to take it away). Use bright colors - too much white in the color tends to mask or cloud the black detail from the photocopy. Let dry between coats and apply as many coats as desired in the colors of choice.

The following products were used for this project: Paper Maché Hexagon Clear Dome Box from Decorator and Craft Corp., Delta Spring Florals Instant Gilded Accents, Delta Ceramcoat Acrylic Paints, Delta Clear Faux Glaze Base, Delta Soft Tints, Delta Satin Decoupage Medium, Delta Matte Interior Spray Varnish, Delta Gloss Exterior Varnish.

Materials:

Paper maché hexagon clear dome box
Acrylic paints: Chocolate Cherry, Moroccan Red
Tints: Leaf Green, Rouge, Royal Blue, Burnt Umber, Light Brown, Orange
Antiquing gel: Warm Brown
Instant Gilded Accents: Spring Florals
Clear glaze base
Satin decoupage medium
Matte interior spray varnish
Gloss exterior varnish
Sponge brush
Plastic wrap
Palette
Brayer (optional)

Nancy's Advanced Project

Bride's Lingerie Box

A special gift box for a very special occasion. The Stencil Magic Roses and Lilacs are the perfect choice for the bridal motif.

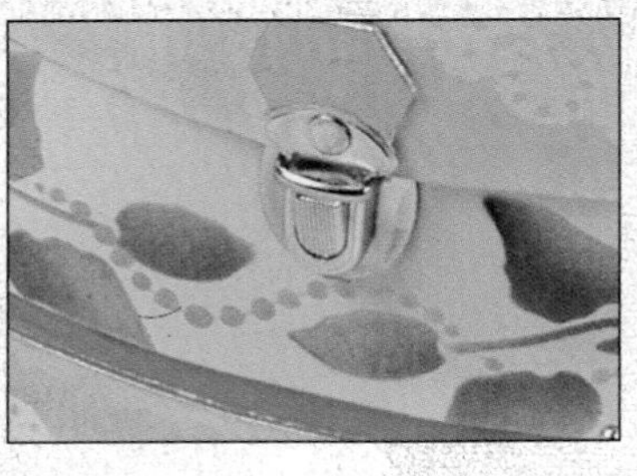

Instructions:

1. Basecoat the outside of the box and lid with Raw Linen. Repeat if necessary. Mix Pink Parfait and Coral and paint on the pink stripe around the base of the box inside the box. This may take more than one coat for good coverage. Allow to dry.

2. Mist the back side of the doily with stencil adhesive spray and adhere it to the box lid. Be sure all the cutouts are pushed out.

3. Use the 5/8" brush to stencil over the entire doily with gold stencil creme. When stenciling, use only a small amount of paint and pull it into the open area of the stencil with a circular motion. Remove the paper doily carefully.

4. Cut the doily into quarters and position the quarters around the rim of the box. Repeat the stenciling procedure in step 3. Remove the doily pieces and apply them around the bottom edge of the box. Stencil as you did in step 3 and remove the doily pieces.

5. Use only the rose, stems, and leaves of the Lilacs and Roses stencil. Position the rose on the upper right side of the box lid. Cover the lilacs portion of the stencil with tape. Add more leaves and stems to fill voids and to make it more pleasing. Stencil the rose with Coral and the tips of the petals with Snow White to soften the color.

6. Stencil the rose leaves with Garden Green, then shade them with Christmas Green. Randomly add tints of Coral to the leaves to add interest. Stencil the stems with Amber.

7. Use a pencil to draw the string for the beads. Make nice large loops at the base of the rose and let them wrap loosely around the stems. Dip the wooden handle of a paintbrush in Gold paint and apply three dots. Dip the brush handle again and apply more dots as desired.

8. Stencil leaves and stems around the box above the pink stripe. Use Garden Green and shade with Christmas Green.

9. Pencil in the string for the beads and apply dots of Gold paint as in step 6.

10. Let dry thoroughly and mist with satin varnish.

11. Make the handle from braid and gold wired beads twisted together and knotted inside the case. Make the bow with 1-5/8"-wide sheer nylon ribbon.

The following products were used for this project: Paper Maché Box from Decorator and Craft Corp., Delta Stencil Magic Roses and Lilacs Stencil #952510018, Delta Stencil Adhesive Spray, Delta Top Coat Spray Varnish, Delta Stencil Paint Cremes, Delta Ceramcoat Gleams.

Materials:

13" round hinged paper maché box
12" round paper doily
Stencils: Roses and Lilacs
Stencil adhesive spray
Spray varnish
Metallic or jewel tone paints: 14K Gold, Raw Linen, Pink Parfait, Coral
Stencil paint creme: Coral, Garden Green, Snow White, Amber, Basic Black, Christmas Green
(3) 3/8" stencil brushes
5/8" stencil brush
Sponge brush
Palette
Masking tape
Ribbon, cord, and decorative accents as desired for handle

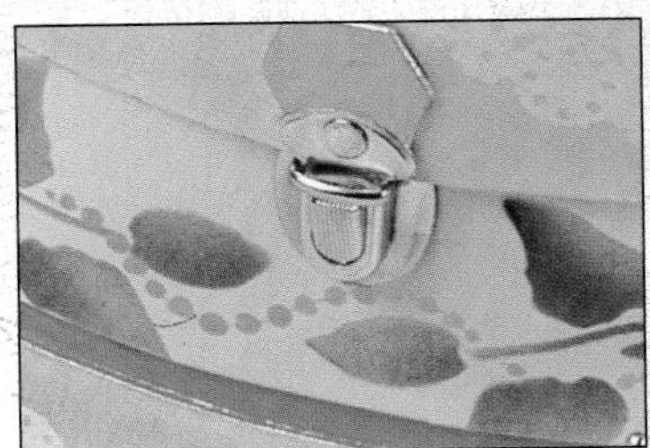

Just for Him

This paper maché box is a perfect personalized gift wrap for any man. By simply changing the tissue paper and colors, it can be adapted for anyone.

Billie's Beginner Project

Billie Worrell

Billie has been a member of the Delta Designer Force since 1992 and has taught seminars and workshops across the country. Her involvement and love for decorative painting and designing are a very important part of her life and she loves to share her ideas.

Instructions:

1. Basecoat the box bottom, inside, edge of top, and the four ball knobs with Payne's Grey paint.

2. Choose a tissue paper in a masculine pattern with a background color very close to the natural color of the paper maché box. If you prefer a light background color, choose a paint color to match and paint the box top and bottom. Cut one piece of tissue paper approximately 2" larger than the box top and another 2" larger than the bottom. Wad the tissue paper in a ball and press it out flat, leaving in the wrinkles.

3. Brush an even coat of decoupage medium on the box top and immediately press on the tissue paper. Brush a light coat of decoupage medium on top of the tissue. Apply tissue paper to the box sides in the same way, working one side at a time. Let it dry completely and trim the edges.

4. Place the last initial of the monogram stencil in the center of the box lid. Tear a small piece of stencil sponge and place it in the clip of the Stencil Buddy. Load the sponge with Payne's Grey paint, remove the excess on a palette, and stencil with a light pouncing motion. Position the first and middle initials of the monogram stencils on the front side of the box. Repeat the stenciling procedure.

5. Brush satin varnish on the entire box and the four wood ball knobs. Let dry.

6. Glue the ball knobs to the bottom of the box for feet.

The following products were used for this project: Decorator & Craft Corp. Paper Maché Box #28-0014, Walnut Hollow Wood Ball Knobs, Delta Acrylic Paint, Delta Decoupage Medium, Delta Monogram Magic Stencils, Delta Stencil Buddy and Stencil Sponge, Delta Sobo Premium Craft & Fabric Glue, Delta Satin Varnish.

Materials:

7-1/2" square paper maché box
4 wood ball knobs, 1-1/4"
1 sheet standard size tissue paper
Acrylic paint: Payne's Grey
Satin decoupage medium
Monogram stencils
Stencil Buddy
Stencil sponge
Craft glue
Satin varnish
1" wash/glaze acrylic paintbrush
Scissors
Palette

Billie's Intermediate Project

Romantic

Simple leaves and roses on a crackled and antiqued soft background give an aged and romantic flair to this project. It would make a lovely gift box for Valentine's Day or any occasion.

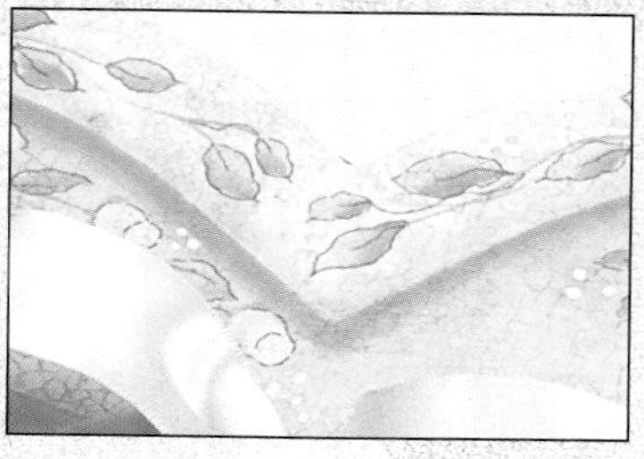

Instructions:

Pattern on page 123

1. Use the compass to lightly mark a 1" border around the top edge of the box lid.

2. Use the 1" wash brush to basecoat the lid sides and under the rim with Oasis Green paint. Basecoat inside the border line with Mello Yellow. Basecoat the border of the box lid and the box bottom with Rose Petal Pink.

3. Trace the design on tracing paper and transfer it to the box using transfer paper and a stylus. Don't transfer any portion of the design that is not absolutely necessary. It's better to use the design as a guide and freehand the project.

4. Painting the design: Both the leaves and rose are painted with both sizes of double-loaded shader brushes. Dampen the brush in water, blot it on a paper towel, load one side in one color and other side in a second color and blend the colors on a palette. The roses are Rose Petal Pink and Hydrangea Pink. Place the Rose Petal Pink at the top of the rose and use a wiggle motion stroke (the Hydrangea Pink will create the shading). Reload the brush and place the Rose Petal Pink to the side of the top, press and pull to the other side using a "c" stroke for the bowl of the rose. Only two strokes are needed. The leaves are done with a double-load of Oasis Green and Rose Petal Pink on the Mello Yellow background and in Oasis Green and Hydrangea Pink on the pink border. Load the brush in the two colors and blend on the palette. Place the chisel edge at the tip of the leaf, pull slightly, press, and lift (basically an "s" stroke). Keep the pink to the top of the leaves and the green to the bottom. Freehand the border design (refer to the photo). Thin Oasis Green paint with water and use the liner brush to paint tendrils at the base of the rose and stems.

Materials:

Paper maché heart-shaped box
2 yards pink wire edge ribbon, 1-1/2"-wide
Acrylic paints: Oasis Green, Mello Yellow, Rose Petal Pink, Hydrangea Pink
Color Float
Fine Crackle Finish Steps 1 & 2
Brown antiquing gel
Satin varnish
Brushes:
- *1" wash/glaze*
- *#8 flat shader*
- *#12 flat shader*
- *#1 liner*
- *1" sponge brush*

Compass with pencil
Stylus
Brown Identi-Pen
Tracing and transfer paper
Palette
Paper towels

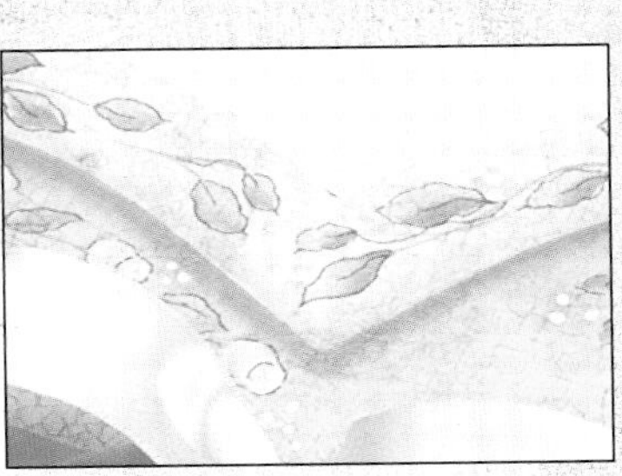

5. Add Color Float to clean water (one drop per ounce of water). Dip the brush in the mixture, blot on a paper towel, side load with Oasis Green paint, blend on a palette, and float around the inner border of the heart. Let all paints dry completely.

6. To crackle and antique the box, use the wash brush to apply an even coat of Step 1 Crackle Finish. Let dry and apply Step 2. Let dry for several hours. Fine cracks will appear as Step 2 dries. Use the sponge brush to apply brown antiquing gel and wipe it off immediately, leaving it in the fine cracks only. Let dry overnight.

7. To add detail: Lightly go over the roses to lighten if needed. Outline the rose and leaves with the brown Identi-Pen and add additional stems. Use the stylus and add small dots of the two shades of pinks around the design and small dots of Mello Yellow to the centers of the roses.

8. Apply a coat of satin varnish to the entire box.

9. Run the ribbon through the slots on the box and tie a simple bow on top.

The following products were used for this project: Decorator & Craft Corp. Paper Maché Heart Ribbon Tie Box #28-0190, Delta Acrylic Paint, Delta Color Float, Delta Fine Crackle Finish Steps 1 & 2, Delta Brown Antiquing Gel, Delta Satin Varnish, Sakura Identi-Pen #441.

Enlarge 200%

Billie's Advanced Project

A Special Wedding

This decoupage wedding gift box was designed with little pockets to hold something extra and personal on the outside of the box.

Instructions:

1. Use the wash brush to basecoat Seashell White on the box and lid interior, box bottom, and the outer rim of the lid.

2. Starting at the top of the Pink Rose Wedding paper, measure and mark three 6-1/2" high and 12" long pieces of the decorative paper to cover the box sides (this will allow for overlapping as you adhere the paper around the box). Don't use longer pieces of paper or you'll have trouble keeping the paper straight as you work around the box. To make a piece to cover the lid, trace around the lid on the back of the paper and cut out the circle.

3. Brush decoupage medium on the top of the box lid and on the back of the paper circle. Place the paper circle on the box lid and smooth out any wrinkles with your fingers, working from the center out. Brush a coat of medium on top of the paper. Apply the 6-1/2" x 12" pieces around the box in the same way.

4. Working from the bottom of the Pink Rose Wedding paper sheet, cut out individual designs to decoupage. Cut out one complete fan and one postcard to use for the pockets.

5. Use decoupage medium to adhere the ribbon around the rim. Apply some of the paper designs to the sides of the box, working one piece at a time and overlapping 1/4" to 1/2" where the paper pieces meet. Trim away all excess paper.

6. Brush decoupage medium on the backs of the remaining paper designs (including the fan and postcard). Adhere these on the bristol board and apply a coat of decoupage medium on top of the designs. Let dry and cut out.

7. Slightly bend the fan cutout, curving backwards, and apply decoupage medium to the edges and bottom of the fan. Adhere to the side of the box where desired to form a pocket.

8. Stick foam dots on the backs of the medium and large size flower designs on bristol board and use decoupage medium to adhere them to the box as desired. Bend them slightly for a more natural look. Use the medium to adhere additional small flowers to the sides and around the box rim on top of the ribbon. Use decoupage medium to adhere the bottom edge of the postcard to the box lid, bending it slightly forward to form another pocket. Build up around the bottom and sides of the postcard with additional flowers and a bow. Let the box dry completely.

9. Brush two or more coats of gloss varnish on the entire box, including the bottom and interior. Let dry between coats.

10. Place something special or personal in the pockets. I chose silk roses and an antique handkerchief.

The following products were used for this project: Decorator & Craft Corp. Paper Maché Hat Box #28-0065B, Finmark Pink Rose Wedding Paper #08 by Artifacts, Delta Acrylic Paint, Delta Decoupage Medium, Delta Gloss Varnish.

Materials:

10" round paper maché box
19-1/2" x 27" Pink Rose Wedding Paper
1 yard pink satin ribbon, 1"-wide
11" x 14" bristol board
Self-adhesive foam dots, 1/4" thick
Acrylic paint: Seashell White
Gloss exterior varnish
1" wash/glaze brush
Scissors
Ruler
Palette
Paper towels

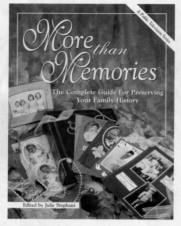

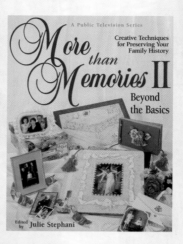

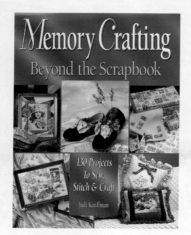

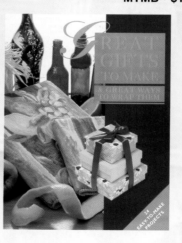

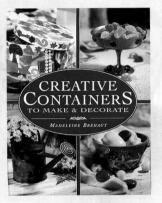

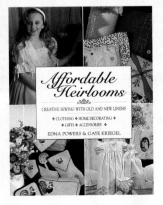